3rd Teddy Bear & friends® Price Guide

by Helen Sieverling

European values furnished by Lorraine Freisberg

Bear on carrousel horse: **Hermann,** 20in (51cm) tall. c.1950, glass eyes, jointed arms and legs, swivel head, straw stuffed. No mark. Excellent condition. **$375-up** £200 DM500. Bear ticket taker: **Hermann,** 23in (58cm) tall, c.1948, glass eyes, jointed arms and legs, swivel head, straw stuffed. Gold metal button reads "Hermann//Teddy//Original." Excellent condition. **$425-up** £150 DM500. Bear ticket giver: **Hermann,** 13in (33cm), c.1930, *The Helen Sieverling Bear,* glass eyes, jointed arms and legs, swivel head, straw stuffed. No mark. Excellent condition. **$500** £80 to 120 DM250 to 400. Carrousel Horse, unknown maker, horse has glass eyes. **$3,000**

Published by Hobby House Press Cumberland, Maryland 21502

Dedication

To my beloved parents — my darling mother, Mrs. Mabel May, and to the cherished memory of my late dad, the Reverend R. Leslie May, I lovingly dedicate this book.

In Appreciation ...

I wish to express my sincere appreciation to the following people without whose contributions and assistance this Price Guide would not be possible.

Gary Anderson, John Axe, Doris E. Beck, Frances Benson, Elke Block, Kathleen Bonewitz, Catherine Bordi, Annalisse-Marie Bowers, Samuel Glenn Bowers, Shirley Boyington, Bernie Crampton, Elizabeth A. Dahle, Denise Dewire, Stephen Eberhart, Tatum Egelin, Jayne Lee Elliott, Jerry and Bill Elliott, Cathy Faigle, Robert H. Gaither, M.D., Diane Gard, Russell B. Gorman, Laura Lee Greene, Jane Hamilton, Miles Hamilton, Betty Hansen, Mimi Hiscox, Donna Hodges, Jo Ann Ingraham, Werner Keck, Bundy Kinder, Jeanne King (Bear Kingdom), Gerry Klein, Norma G. Knox, Pauline Kulp, Linda K. Lilley, Wendy Lockwood, Harold J. Lotz, Lynn Lumley (Grandma Lynn's Teddy Bears) Flora Mediate (Flora's Teddys), Doris and Terry Michaud, Charlene Nelson, Vera Oliver, Nancy and Paul Permakoff, Donna Pulliam, Deborah Ratliff, Deborah Ritchey, Rick K. Saxman, Patricia N. Schoonmaker, Steve Schutt, Sarah Ann Sieverling, Barbara Sixby, Venita Smith, Marilyn P. Stephenson, Cordy Strand, Gwyneth A. Taylor, H.E. Thompson, Bonnie Tyree, Lisa M. Vought, Pauline Weis (We're Bears), Joanne D. Wilson, Bette Wolf, Richard Wright Antiques, Sherryl Shirran.

It is with special appreciation and thanks that I mention the following people:

My husband, Glenn Sieverling, for all of his assistance and photography. My Editor, Donna H. Felger. A. Christian Revi, Consulting Editor and Carolyn Cook, Managing Editor, for their special help. Kerry Murray, for helping in every way possible. Peter and Anna Kalinke of Ohio, for helping in many, many ways. Susan Bowers, my secretary. My Publisher, Gary R. Ruddell, for all his kindness and patience without whom this book could not have become a reality.

The 2nd Teddy Bear & friends "Certificate of Registration" #TX1781671 is in the Library of Congress.

Additional copies of this book may be purchased at $9.95 plus $1.25 per copy for postage
from
HOBBY HOUSE PRESS, INC.
900 Frederick Street, Cumberland, Maryland 21502
or from your favorite bookstore or dealer.

Unknown Maker   c1907

8in (20cm) high Teddy Bear Purse
Brown fur; chatelaine clip from which
3 ivory slates extend in fan fashion for
note taking; silver top embossed &
chased with a bird & flowers; shoe-
button eyes.

Excellent condition.

No mark.   **$200-up**
£ 100-150
300-400 DM

Unknown Maker   c1935

3in (8cm) tall,
3in (8cm) long Toy Duck
Tin; yellow head, tail & wings; red
dress; white apron; painted eyes; on
wooden wheels.

Mint condition.

No mark.   **$10**

Verhana (Spain) c1950
  15in tall Hurdy-Gurdy
  Natural wood; tiny flowers &
  children painted on front &
  sides; activated when wound
  with crank on side; marked,
  "Patentado//REIG//Made in
  Spain//Music by Rieg."
  $450-up
(Shown with Schuco Orangutan and
Bear; see pages 120 and 126 for
descriptions.)

Wolverine Supply & Mfg. Co.
  c1930
  13in tall Merry-Go-Round
  Tin; "Made in U.S.A."
  Excellent condition.
  $150-up
(Shown with Character Bear; see page
57 for description.)

F. W. Woolnough   c1930
14in (36cm) Bear (*)
(*) Pooh. Gold mohair;
matching paw pads; shoe-
button eyes; jointed legs &
arms; swivel head; straw
stuffing.
Good condition.
No mark.   **$175-up**

About the Author

Helen Sieverling was born and raised in Kansas. Her father was a minister, and she remembers a happy, glowing childhood growing up in church parsonages. She graduated from high school in Neodesha, Kansas, and attended her church college in Kansas. Her childhood memories are cherished ones with loving parents and two sisters. Teddy Bears and dolls were then, and are now, an integral part of her life..

Her husband, Glenn Sieverling, assists her with her books and does the greater share of the beautiful photography seen in her books and articles. Mrs. Sieverling is a feature writer for *Teddy Bear and friends,* and her *2nd The Teddy Bear & friends Price Guide* is in the Library of Congress.

Mrs. Sieverling receives correspondence from collectors in almost every state in the Union, and from six foreign countries where her books have been read and consulted. This correspondence usually includes requests for her to identify and evaluate Teddy Bears and other plush toy animals. Invariably, the people writing to her mention her articles and price guide, and tell her how much help they have received from them.

Mrs. Sieverling is a member of the International Doll Academy, a prestigious group of people including authors, curators, doll artists, lay people, owners of toy centers and her publisher, Gary R. Ruddell. IDA, as it is known, selects nominees for the coveted DOTY (Doll of the Year) Awards. These nominees are then voted upon by the public at locations all over the United States and through ballots published in *Doll Reader* magazine. She is constantly being asked to speak and share her knowledge of Teddy Bears at conventions and local clubs across the nation.

Teddy Bears are universally loved and, according to Mrs. Sieverling, people who collect them are loving, caring and sharing individuals.

Table of Contents

How To Use This Book

    This price guide has been arranged alphabetically by manufacturer's name. The toy animals, too, have been listed in alphabetical order under the manufacturer's name, and as much as possible in date sequence with the earliest of their type followed by later examples. An asterisk (*) indicates that there is either some special feature about the toy or its proper name has been given.

Values

    Teddy bears and other plush animals are eagerly sought after by collectors the world over. The buying and selling of these collectables between West Germany, England and the United States has increased to such intensity that European collector value ranges are now given by Lorraine Freisberg, a noted dealer in teddy bears and other plush animals. The Deutsch Mark and Pounds Sterling values noted were established from European auctions and antique fairs and not merely currency translations of American collector values. Deutsch Mark or Pounds Sterling values are not given in some categories, such as artist bears, which are unique to American taste.

Introduction

Teddy Bears and other collectible soft toys are being sought after by avid long-time collectors as well as the new collectors who are entering this field daily. Their numbers are growing by leaps and bounds.

This book is written with the greater number of collectors in mind. They may be from the United States, Europe or from the "land down under." They can also be found in remote places in Alaska or in the jungles of South America.

This information guide was conceived not only to establish values compiled from actual buying and selling prices, but to impart and share knowledge of the worth of your soft toy collectibles or, perhaps, one you wish to buy or sell. We do not set prices, nor do we manipulate or distort them. Accuracy is important to us and we strive for it.

In most cases I have been privileged to personally study each collectible pictured and priced in this book. I am pleased to include in this edition the new artist bears that have become so popular in recent years. Collectors have a real appreciation for the artists' handiwork. I have met artist bear makers from coast to coast and they are craftsmen who devote their best efforts and skills to the world of collecting. The modern day artists are striving for and achieving charm and realistic take-me-home-with-you appeal, as well as beautiful objects of art. We welcome their contribution into the realm of values.

Many collectors yearn for at least one or two antique bears for their collections, but for the most part the trend is towards toys they played with as children. Since the greater number of collectors are familiar with toys from 1945 to 1965, which were their playthings, we have concentrated largely on this time slot. The period after World War II became that time in history when many Teddy Bear and soft toy manufacturers were again setting the wheels in motion to produce huggable toys for children. In this period after the war, it was difficult to obtain mohair. Many manufacturers turned to other materials—cotton, rayon, even wood fibers, but mohair was the natural choice for our beloved Teddies. This still holds true today.

A bit of American history is unfolded in this book. A collector brought forth a toy version of one of the 16 Chinook dogs that Admiral Richard Byrd took on his expedition to Alaska in 1928. The Mastiff blood in the Chinook is believed by some to date back to the time of the pharaohs of Egypt.

Another piece of Americana which came to us for sharing and evaluation was an important Eskimo doll with a bisque face. The body was covered with white fur suggesting a rabbit doll. The *Collector's Encyclopedia of Dolls, Volume II,* by the Colemans states: "Interest in these Eskimo dolls was increased by the notoriety about Peary's daughter. . . ." Her name was Marie Ahnighto Peary, born in 1893. The authors further stated: "Sometimes these same dolls and large ears attached to the top of their heads to represent bunnies."

To realize that you own a collectible that had even the remotest place in history brings a joy only a collector can understand.

Editor's note: The values in English Pounds Sterling and West German

Deutsch Marks found in this book were compiled by Lorraine Freisberg, a Teddy Bear collector and dealer living in West Germany. As with most collectibles, prices vary from one location to another. Adding these European values to this price guide enlarges its worth to collectors who are going abroad to buy soft toy animals. It also makes European buyers and sellers aware of values here in the United States.

Ideal Teddy Bear 11in (28cm) tall, c.1910. Tan Mohair with flannel paw pads, shoe button eyes, jointed arms and legs, straw stuffed. No mark. Good condition. **$295-up. £150-200. 300-500 DM.**

Reflections

Let's walk back into the corridors of time. Our country — much younger then, was getting her feet firmly planted on the ground. In 1902, when President McKinley was assassinated, a strong-hearted Vice President, Theodore Roosevelt, firmly took the helm of America and became our beloved 26th President at the age of 42 years. He was the youngest man, then and now, to lead this great country. He was the first American to win the Nobel Peace Prize for his efforts in ending the Russo-Japanese War. He built the Panama Canal, and was the greatest conservationist among all of our Presidents. You have only to travel to Mount Rushmore to see his likeness carved there along with three other great American Presidents.

In his birthplace in New York City can be found a room devoted to the history of the Teddy Bear. Theodore Roosevelt was born October 27, 1858, and if he could know the love and admiration the Teddy Bear and doll worlds hold for him in their hearts, he would be overwhelmed. We all love the story of this great man and have proclaimed him to be the father of our beloved Teddy bears. Time has shown that in the world of dolls, too, there is much warmth and respect for this great American hero. Let us consider a few of the dolls inspired by this fine President.

In 1908, the well-known Schoenhut Teddy Roosevelt doll was made. They are scarce today and much sought after. The years from 1908 to 1910 are remembered as the time of Roosevelt's Great African Hunting Trip. This doll depicts the President in hunting garb, and as the main figure in the whole Schoenhut safari set.

According to *Doll News* (August 1965), the official publication of the United Federation of Doll Clubs, a patent was applied for in 1910 by Frank C.A. Richardson of Springfield, Massachusetts, covering a cloth doll depicting an African native, 14½in (37cm) tall, which was made of black stockinette material. This doll had fur hair, shoe button eyes, and had brass rings firmly sewn in as earrings and a nose ring. The loin cloth it wore was made of real leopard skin sewn onto a red wool felt band. The wrist, arm and ankle bracelets it wore were made of gold colored metal with floral engraved designs. The choker beads around its neck were also gold colored metal with a longer strand of old looking beads. The shoe button eyes had a white cloth covered metal backing.

The female native doll was also shown in the patent and was a shorter doll, 10½in (27cm) tall. Her raffia-type grass skirt was attached to a red cotton band and covered her brown printed panties. All the beads, wristlets and necklaces were made of old glass beads, and her eyes and facial features were embroidered. The girl's hair was made of heavy black lace over stuffing, giving her a high appearance.

In 1914, several doll firms, one of which was Electra, manufactured dolls representing various characters — Uncle Sam Liberty Dolls, and so forth. One dressed in khaki clothing slightly resembled Teddy Roosevelt. The dolls were crudely made and their cotton bodies were stuffed with excelsior. These dolls were helpers to the President and considered as "Poctors."

Schoenhut Teddy Roosevelt doll.

In 1983, the House of Nisbet made a wonderful Teddy Roosevelt doll holding a small Teddy bear in his arms. The doll is authentically dressed, complete with tiny Teddy Roosevelt eyeglasses. This doll was made to commemorate the President's 125th birthday. The Effanbee Doll Company has also recently made a wonderful commemorative Teddy Roosevelt doll.

The contribution this beloved President made to the doll and Teddy Bear world, though inadvertently, is overwhelming. It would appear this great President, unknowingly, has reached into our realm to spread joy and happiness in our day.

Left: Black cloth doll patented by C.A. Richardson in 1910.

Right: Electra Teddy Roosevelt Doll.

Opposite page: House of Nisbet Teddy Roosevelt Doll.

Ideal electric-eyed bear, c1907-1927.

Notes About the Manufacturers and Characteristics of Their Bears

In the early 1900s, American and European manufacturers were feverishly producing Teddy Bears to meet the toy market's demands. Many of the bears had identification tags or, if dressed, possibly tags on their clothes. Much to the chagrin of present-day collectors, these identifying tags were often removed and now present a problem when trying to assign a bear to a certain maker.

What follows is a brief history of some of the major Teddy Bear manufacturers and some characteristics peculiar to those bears that they made.

Ideal

There were 12 American companies in full swing at the height of the popularity of the Teddy Bear. The Ideal Novelty & Toy Co., which lays claim for making the first American bear, also produced the *Shirley Temple* and many other highly collectible dolls.

A 1903 Teddy Bear, one of the first Ideal Teddies, now resides in the Smithsonian Institution — a very important piece of Americana. The early American Teddy Bears, and especially the early Ideals, are avidly sought by American Teddy Bear collectors today. The Ideal bear is a part of our heritage and is as American as the 4th of July.

The span of time since the Michtoms made their first bear and lovingly placed it in their candy store window has been more than three quarters of a century. Time has surrendered to that simple love and happiness the lowly Teddy Bear

brings to the hearts and minds of children and collectors everywhere. The army of Teddy Bear collectors today stands overwhelmingly near the top of whatever (you name it) collectors are collecting today.

Along with Teddy Bears and dolls, this remarkable firm has manufactured molded plastic playthings. The joy and happiness this company has brought to children around the Christmas tree each year since the first Teddy Bear was hand-stuffed with excelsior can never be measured.

When you look into the face of an Ideal bear, you immediately realize it is triangular with oversized ears and, if they are originally sewn, they will be just ever so slightly back of the center of the head and sewn in a slightly curved line to give an even more triangular look to the head.

Rather than sewing the nose with embroidery floss, the nose may be a solid piece of fabric as is the one in the Smithsonian. The mohair usually is bristly and sometimes the gold tones on the bears can be harsh. There are a few white ones in collections, and only very occasionally a black or brown.

Berg Bears

The Berg Company is located in the Tyrolean countryside of Austria. This company has made Teddy Bears and soft toys since the end of World War II.

Berg's trademark is "Tiere mit Herz" (Animals with Heart), and usually you will find a red metal heart attached to the

Teddy or soft toy as part of its identification, as well as a label sewn in one of the seams.

The Berg bears are of good workmanship, fine quality fabric, glass eyes and plenty of appeal for collectors of fine Teddy Bears and soft toys.

If you find an early Teddy Bear, it may have a label in the seam of the left ear which reads: "BERG" on one side and "SCHUTZ" along with their logo on the other side.

Berg bears have medium length arms and long, narrow feet. Their noses turn up ever so slightly and they have plenty of appeal.

Gund

Adolph Gund came to America from Germany in 1898. He became the founder-father of Gund, Inc., and gave it his name. He was joined in 1910 by J. Swedlin, who purchased the company in 1923.

Gund is a family business. The daughter of J. Swedlin, whose name is Rita Raiffe, is head of the firm today. The family prefers to keep it as a small family business rather than build it into a large corporation.

From 1930 to 1960, Gund manufactured stuffed animals for Walt Disney. Gund and Disney created many of the Disney characters that are so popular with collectors today. Disney manufactures their own creations today.

Many collectors love and collect the Winnie-the-Pooh, made by Gund for Sears stores. The Pooh bears are still being made for Sears by the Gund company.

Gund Teddy Bears and soft toys are made with great care and follow safety standards so they may be loved by children as well as collectors.

The Gund company made the wonderful Bialosky bears which are treasured by many Teddy Bear and soft toy collectors.

Gebrüder Hermann

The Gebr. Hermann KG, Hermann Teddy Plüschspielwarenfabrik of Germany really had its beginning in 1907 when Johann Hermann, grandfather of Artur and Werner Hermann (formerly managers of the company) began making Teddy Bears.

Bernhard Hermann, Johann's eldest son, was sent to Meiningen, Germany, for a part of his trade and business education. He returned to work for his father's business until 1911, when he established his own business. In 1912, he and his wife moved to Sonneberg where they started manufacturing dolls and Teddy Bears, thus the slogan, "Your bear maker in Germany since 1911." Sonneberg was at that time the world's center for toy making. Not only were many toy factories in operation, but many American toy purchasers such as Woolworth, Kresge, Borgfeldt and Wolf & Sons, to name a few, had export houses there as well. All of these firms obtained toys from Bernhard Hermann and sold them in America.

In 1948, Bernhard Hermann and his sons relocated the business from the German Democratic Republic to Hirschaid, near Bamberg, in the American Zone of Germany. Artur headed up the finances and sales, and Werner designed the Teddy Bears and saw to it that the highest quality of Teddy Bear making was upheld in the Hermann bears.

The Hermann bears are bought, loved and treasured by Teddy Bear collectors all over the world, wherever they are sold. Margit Hermann Drohlshagen and Marion Hermann Mehling now fill important roles in the Hermann company.

A few good tips to keep in mind in identifying a Hermann bear is that more often than not, only three toes and nails were embroidered on the paw pads. Sometimes, there is no seam under the arms, only in front and in back. The black floss nose is sometimes elongated stitches on each end rather than even stitching. The company identifies their bears with tags and medallions which are a delight to collectors.

| 1911—1929 | 1930—1939 | 1940—1951 | since 1952 |

Marks and tags used by Gebrüder Hermann from 1911 to the present.

Gold mohair bear by Hermann, c1940.

The Hermann Plush Company
Hermann-Spielwaren GmbH

There is another firm in West Germany with the Hermann name. It is not to be confused with the GEbr. Hermann name we know so well. They all have the same great-grandfather, Johann Hermann, but these Hermanns are descendants of Max Hermann. These are two different firms.

The Hermann Plush Company is headed by Mr. Rolf Hermann. The factory is located in Cottendorf near Neustadt, Germany. This company is presently engaged in the making of a complete line of Teddy Bears and soft toy products. Some Teddy Bears have made their way to America and are in collections.

In the *2nd Teddy Bear & Friends Price Guide,* on page 14 (above left), one of these bears is pictured with a nice view of their identification tag which represents their company. They also have a tag which is green and silver foil and is easily distinguishable. This latter tag motif shows a Teddy Bear leading a dog.

Knickerbocker

The Knickerbocker Toy Company had its beginning in 1850, in Albany, New York. Their first toys were lithographed alphabet blocks.

After the turn of the century, when the Teddy Bear came into being, this firm joined others in turning out Teddy Bears. They also made many other soft animal toys.

In the 1960s, they produced many Smokey Bears, including one which talks on tape and says eight different sentences. This company is no longer in existence.

Characteristics of this company's bear is a separately sewn-in muzzle and the paw pads were more often than not made of velveteen. The feet were not well de-fined. Arms were short. The mohair was always top quality. Their slogan was, "Toys of Distinction."

Merrythought

Merrythought Limited calls Shropshire, England, home and it is there many wonderful Teddy Bears and soft toys have been born in the beautiful English countryside since 1930. In 1919, Mr. W.G. Holmes, along with Mr. G.H. Laxton, were engaged in the business of manufacturing mohair. It was c1930 when Merrythought toys were made, such as those Florence Atwood designed for this company until her death in 1949. Mr. Oliver Holmes manages Merrythought today.

The name Merrythought comes from the old English term for a wishbone. When a wishbone is to be pulled apart, each person makes a wish and the wish is supposed to be granted to the lucky person who gets the larger of the two pieces.

To identify a Merrythought without printed identification, you have only to look at the head. From Mr. "Twisty Cheek" to the conventional bears made by them since 1931, they each have a rather classic look about them which all bear collectors love. Some have interesting embroidered claws on their paw pads which extend to the underfoot of the bear. Noses tend to be ever so slightly squared in comparison to the sharp pointed or turned up noses of other bears.

Merrythought Teddy Bears and soft toys are beautifully made. They have wonderful Teddy Bear appeal. Merrythought soft toys are colorful and have a beautiful lifelike quality about them. They are a "must" in every collection.

White mohair bear by Merrythought, c1935.

House of Nisbet

Peggy Nisbet started making dolls in 1953. It was the time of Queen Elizabeth's ascension to the English throne and, of course, her first doll was just that — a ceramic figure of the new Queen.

Jack Wilson is the husband of Alison Nisbet, Peggy's daughter, and both are deeply involved in the Nisbet Company.

The late Peter Bull worked closely with Peggy Nisbet and Jack Wilson in bringing to Teddy Bear collectors the wonderful Bully Bears and also, the 12 Zodiac bears.

The Nisbet bears are easily identified by short pug noses and oversized ears. They are always cuddly and possess plenty of bear appeal and a typically chubby look so familiar to the English bear. Bully Bears have extra long muzzles.

Yes/No Musical Bear by Schuco, c1945.

Dean's Childsplay, Ltd.

This is a subsidiary of Dean's Rag Book Company, Ltd., circa 1903, which printed rag books and dolls, toys, toy animals, birds and other toy figures.

About 1969, they were busily engaged in unique items such as the Trike Boy and the Rabbit on a Tricycle. In 1933, they produced their version of Mickey Mouse. Blinkums was made in 1935 as a nightdress case. Also, Dismal Desmond and Cheerful Desmond were produced the same year.

Through the years, Teddy Bears and soft toys have been made and sold by this firm to the delight of children and, lately, the joy of collectors.

Old Dean's Rag Book items sometimes have a label on the foot which states the name of the company.

Newer items, made from fine British wool, are well marked.

Schuco

In 1912, Heinrich Muller and Heir Schreyer formed "Schreyer and Company," better known to collectors everywhere as "Schuco." Actually, Schuco was meant to be a trademark. Mr. Muller had formerly been associated with the Bing Company.

The first endeavor of the newly formed company was clockwork toys. It was in the 1920s and 1930s that they turned to soft toys.

Collectors everywhere love the yes-no bears, rabbits, ducks and monkeys, many of which are pictured in this price guide.

In the 1970s, many miniature bears and rabbits were exported to America and have made their way into bear collections. The Schuco factory is no longer in business, but the outstanding collectibles they made are highly treasured and most collections feature something this wonderful firm gave us to enjoy.

It might be difficult to identify a large Schuco bear without identification. You should look for a rather sharp nose, arms that are rather short in proportion to the longer legs, beautiful workmanship, large ears, and a small to medium size hump. The miniatures may be made with the plush over a metal frame, many times with metal eyes, but always with a precious "take-me-home-with-you" look.

Steiff

The Steiff Company is a wonderful German firm that has made and sold bears since the so-called Teddy Roosevelt "incident." It is a joy when one can add an early Steiff to his or her collection.

Hans-Otto Steiff and Dr. Herbert Zimmerman have made numerous trips abroad to mingle with collectors everywhere and manufacture Teddies and soft toys to the delight of collectors.

It was over 100 years ago that Margarete Steiff began to make soft toys. She started with a motto which still exists today — "Only the best is good enough for our children."

Richard Steiff, a nephew of Margarete Steiff, designed the first Steiff Teddy Bear, about 1903; it was made of gray mohair which was purchased to make Steiff elephants.

When you pick up an early Steiff bear with no identification tags, you will see very long, slightly curved arms sometimes extending to what we might call the "knees" of the Teddy. Extremely long feet, a pronounced hump and either a "cone-shaped" head or, more often, an ever so slightly "turned up" nose. Steiff bears have "personality plus."

Steiff Buttons and Identification

Elephant, stamped	1898
Orange and red interchangeable tags	1926-1934
Yellow label, printed Steiff	To 1945
U.S. Zone Germany labels	1948-1949
Raised script (Steiff)	1905-1960
Indented script	1960-1980
Large gold button	1981-present

There are a great many wonderful old Teddy Bears and other soft animal toys which have not yet been attributed to a maker. These "unknowns" may have been made by any one of the several German soft toy manufacturers listed on the following pages which were gleaned from the text and illustrations found in the *German Doll Encyclopedia, 1800-1930*, by Jürgen & Marianne Cieslik (published by Hobby House Press, Inc., 1985).

Rare gold mohair bear by Steiff, c1907.

Other German Teddy Bear and Soft Toy Makers

In the book *German Doll Encyclopedia 1800-1939* (Hobby House Press, Inc., 1985) the authors, Jürgen and Marianne Cieslik, mentioned several German manufacturers of Teddy Bears and other soft animal toys, in many instances illustrating their trademarks and original catalog illustrations.

This book contains some very important, heretofore unpublished information about German doll and toy manufacturers, many never heard of before in this country. The following list of toy manufacturers who actually stated they produced Teddy Bears or soft animal toys was gleaned from the pages of this monumental work on the German doll and toy industry. Collectors of both dolls and Teddy Bears will be forever grateful to the Ciesliks for their indepth and careful research in this field of collecting.

Büchner, Oskar, Ebersdorf, Coburg, Germany. Listed as making "Dolls, Store Mannequins, and stuffed toys, circa 1925. This company's trademark consisted of a Teddy Bear within a triangle and the letters, 'O.B.'"

Cresco-Spielwarenfabrik GmbH, Schweinfurt, Bavaria, Germany. Listed "Dancing Dolls, Dancing Harlequins, Dancing Groups and Dancing Teddy Bears," circa 1920.

E. Dehler, Coburg, Germany. Listed as making plush animals, circa 1906. A trade card in the Ciesliks' book illustrated dolls, Teddy Bears, monkeys and rabbits, some of which were dressed, or partially dressed.

Deuerlein, Josef Nachf. (successors to Kohler & Rosenwald), Nuremberg, Germany. Listed as making plush animal toys as early as 1910. In early 1913, this company was reported to be making stuffed toys. Their 1907 trademark included a Teddy Bear and the word "Hercules"; their 1925 catalog featured a Teddy Bear waving a banner emblazoned with the word "Kolundro" leading an elephant which was being ridden by a monkey.

Deutsche Kolonial-Kapok-Werke AG, Berlin, Potsdam and Ergenzigen, Germany. This company's trademark indicated that they made dolls and toy animals; it also featured the likeness of a bulldog.

Dressel & Pietschmann, Coburg, Germany. Two Teddy Bears, a doll and a Santa Claus figure were featured in this company's trademark.

Engelhardt, Hermann & Julius, Sonneberg and Rodach, Germany. Advertised stuffed animal toys and illustrated a rabbit and a puppy in one of their advertisements, circa 1911.

Fleischmann & Bloedel, Sonneberg, Germany; Paris, France; and London, England. In 1914, this company's trademark illustrated a Teddy Bear dancing with a doll.

Fleischmann, Adolf, & Craemer, Sonneberg, Germany. Early photographs of this company's showroom pictured some animal toys. Particular animals featured were a rather fierce leopard and a lion, and a long-eared rabbit. There were also some animal pull-toys on platforms in the photograph.

Förster, Albert, Neustadt, Germany. Their trademark featured a jointed Teddy Bear and their initials, "A.F."

Förster, Gustav, Neustadt, Germany. A catalog page illustrated a seated (and probably jointed) Teddy Bear and a Teddy Bear on wheels.

Gans, Otto, Waltershausen, Germany. This company's trademark, "Kindertraum" (circa 1930), featured a bulldog with a rough collar like those made by Steiff and Gebrüder Hermann during about the same period.

Hahn & Co., Nuremberg, Germany. This company is listed as making plush bears and other stuffed animals, circa 1921. Their trademark, in 1921, featured a Teddy Bear popping out of a world globe.

Harmus, Carl Jr., Sonneberg, Germany. Advertised and illustrated a soft, stuffed, dressed Teddy Bear in 1912. Their trademark, registered in 1909, featured a Teddy Bear holding a doll.

Henze & Steinhäuser, Erfurt and Gehren, Germany. This company advertised woolen animals, plush animals and softly stuffed kapok animals in 1925. In 1927, they advertised "woolen animals." One of the company's trademarks featured the figure of a monkey.

Jügelt, Walter, Coburg, Germany. Their trademark (circa 1924) illustrated a doll and a bear. The firm manufactured dolls and toys.

Kletzin & Co., Heinrich Johann, Leipzig, Germany. This company is listed as making stuffed toys. Their trademark was a cat dressed in a clown costume.

Kohler & Rosenwald (succeeded by Josef Deuerlein), Nuremberg, Germany. This company is listed as makers of stuffed figures. Their trademark was a Teddy Bear waving a flag. The trademark word "Kolundro" was coined from letters taken from their combined names and

was later used as a trademark by their successor, Josef Deuerlein.

Krauth, Werner, Leipzig, Germany. This company's trademark (circa 1920) included a bear dancing around a globe with dressed dolls and a jester. The globe was topped with a representation of an old sailing ship with the initials, "W.K." Since the firm was known to have made dolls and toys, this could indicate that Teddy Bears were among the toys they produced.

Leven & Sprenger, Sonneberg, Germany. A catalog page from 1910 illustrated a jointed Teddy Bear and other plush animal toys. This included a doll-faced plush rooster and a doll dressed in plush Teddy Bear clothing.

Luthardt, Louis Philipp, Neustadt, Germany. This company was listed as a maker of "stuffed bears," circa 1921. Their trademark illustrated a Teddy Bear and a seated doll with letters "P" and "L" in a cipher.

Müller, Andreas, Sonneberg, Germany. Their trademark consisted of a jointed Teddy Bear, a doll and a jester.

Rogner, Hermann, Nachf, Nuremberg, Germany. This company advertised in 1926 that they had a particularly large selection of Teddy Bears.

Schmey, Gustav, Sonneberg, Germany. An illustrated trade card issued for the 1911 Leipzig Fair showed two dogs on wheels, a jointed plush monkey, plush white cat and a Teddy Bear standing on all fours with a chain that extended from his snout to a tree trunk. There was also a plush covered horse, sheep, donkey and a dog which pulled a cart.

Schmidt, Eduard, Coburg, Germany. This company's trademark, circa 1925, illustrated a "Sicora Teddy." This was a smiling, fully-jointed Teddy Bear. The "Sicora Teddy" and a "Sicora Monkey" were illustrated in a German wholesale toy catalog in 1924/1926.

Steiner, Hermann, Neustadt, Germany. An advertisement in a 1926 issue of *Deutsche Spielwarenzeitung,* illustrated "Rolf, The Lovable Teddy Bear."

Strunz, Wilhelm, Nuremberg, Germany. This company was listed as a maker of stuffed animals, circa 1911. Their trademark included the figure of a bear holding a shield containing the initials "W.S."

Wohlmann, Otto, Nuremberg, Germany. Listed as a maker of stuffed toys. Their trademark included the figure of a standing bear and the letters, "OWN."

Zinner, Gottlieb & Söhne, Schalkau, Germany. A catalog dated 1900 illustrated and showed what appeared to be a flocked papier-mâché bear musical toy on a stick.

Taking Care of Your Teddy Bear
and Other Soft Toys

Always handle your soft toys gently and with clean hands. This is one of the best ways to preserve your treasures. If you have ever felt a break in the excelsior stuffing inside your old Teddy's arm, it is probably due to his being picked up by the arm, rather than by gently lifting the entire body with both hands.

Many collectors are interested in preserving and taking the best care of Teddy as possible. If your bear is not soiled and in pristine condition, you need only to brush him gently with a clean, soft brush especially set aside for this use. Always watch for insect damage and try to keep your collectibles in an even temperature. Never store them in plastic bags as this tends to draw moisture. A cedar chest might be the safest place to store them but if you wish to show them to your friends, a cabinet with glass windows and doors would be preferable.

If you own a bear or bunny that needs cleaning, there is a cleaning method I have used with success.

You will need two bowls filled with tap water at room temperature. In one bowl place one-half capful of your favorite wool cleaner. In the other bowl, one-half capful of your favorite conditioner. Be sure to check both to determine that they are indeed gentle to fabrics.

After gently brushing as much loose dirt away from the fur as possible, you are ready to begin. Whip the cleaner with a fork or wisk until there is a lot of foam formed on top. Using **only the foam,** apply a little at a time to the surface of the bear using circular motions and a soft brush. Do not apply water, only the foam, so you do not get the stuffing wet. After you have completely gone over the animal, take a piece of toweling and dip it in the water with the conditioner. Wring out the toweling and very gently go over the entire bear.

With a clean, dry towel, very gently go over the Teddy in a circular motion to absorb any excess moisture. Then let him dry naturally for a clean, shaggy look.

If you follow these directions precisely, you will be delighted with the results. Remember, you clean your treasures at your own risk. Neither Hobby House Press, Inc., nor the author take any responsibility for your treasures.

Acton   c1938
11in (31cm) Bear (*)
(*) Twyford. Long white mohair; brown floss nose; blue felt paw pads; blue glass eyes; jointed legs & arms; swivel head; straw stuffing; cloth tag reads, "Twyford Products made in England by Acton London."
Cloth tag.   Mint condition.   **$175-up**
£ 50-60
200-300 DM

Below:
Aetna   c1907
23in (58cm) Bear
White mohair; shoe-button eyes; jointed legs & arms; swivel head; straw stuffing; rare American bear.
Excellent condition.
No mark.
$1700-up
£ 400-500
1200-1500 DM

Alexander c1953

16in (41cm) Dogs (*)

(*) Poodles, Boy & Girl. Gray poodle cloth accented with dark gray looped yarn; plastic eyes; not jointed; kapok stuffing; tags read, "Madam Alexander//All Rights Reserved//New York, U.S.A."

Mint condition.

Cloth tags. **$300-up (pair)**

Below left:

Applause 1985

22in (56cm) Bear (*)

(*) Huckleberry — Set #1. Gray synthetic mohair; wooden face & paw pads; red & white checked shirt; denim overalls; #297 of 7500.

Paper tag. Mint condition. **$225-up**

Below right:

Applause 1985

(Robert Raikes)

16in (41cm) Bear (*)

(*) Bently — Set #1. Brown synthetic mohair; wooden muzzle, face & paw pads; plastic eyes; jointed legs & arms; swivel head; synthetic stuffing; black & maroon checked vest; #2053 of 7500.

Paper tag. Mint condition. **$275-up**

Applause 1985
(Robert Raikes)
　　　　16in (41cm) Bear (*)
(*) Eric — Set #1. Light brown synthetic mohair; plastic eyes; jointed legs
& arms; swivel head; modern stuffing;
blue knitted costume; ''Robert
Raikes'' knitted on scarf; #2599 of
7500.　　Mint condition.　　**$475-up**

Below left:
Applause 1985
(Robert Raikes)
　　　　21in (53cm) Bear (*)
(*) Sebastian — Set #. 1 Synthetic
mohair; wooden face & paw pads;
plastic eyes; jointed legs & arms;
swivel head; synthetic stuffing;
checked vest; bow tie; wire-rimmed
glasses; #1364 of 7500.
Paper tag.　　Mint condition.　　**$250-up**

Below right:
Applause 1986
(Robert Raikes)
　　　　16in (41cm) Bear (*)
(*) Christopher — Set #2. Synthetic
mohair; wooden muzzle, face & paw
pads; plastic eyes; jointed legs & arms;
swivel head; synthetic stuffing; sailor
costume.
Paper tag.　　Mint condition.　　**$300-up**

Applause 1987
(Robert Raikes)
16in (41cm) Bear (*)
(*) Casey — Set #4. Cream synthetic mohair; plastic eyes; jointed legs & arms; swivel head; synthetic stuffing; baseball uniform; #21 of 7500.
Mint condition.
Paper tag. **$150-up**

Applause 1986
(Robert Raikes)
16in (41cm) Bear (*)
(*) Penelope — Set #2. Beige synthetic mohair; wooden face & paw pads; plastic eyes; jointed legs & arms; swivel head; modern stuffing; pink dress; #6781 of 15,000.
Mint condition.
Signed on foot. **$525-up**

Ruth Ann DeWitt c1986
    11in (28cm) Rabbit
    Pink mohair; pink ultra
    suede inner ears & foot paw
    pads; black floss nose &
    mouth; pink glass eyes;
    jointed legs; swivel head.
        Mint condition.
Cloth tag. **$60-up**

Below:
Joan Adams c1986
(S'Bear Change)
    8in (20cm) Bear
    4in (10cm) Horse
    Ivory lamb's wool bear;
    white dralon horse with
    black spots, boa feather
    mane & tail; plastic eyes; not
    jointed; modern stuffing; tag
    on bear reads, "Little Bear
    Riding Hood."
        Mint condition.
Paper tags. **$120-up (set)**

Above left:
Linda Ashcroft c1987
(Woolieland)
14in (36cm) Cat (*)
(*) Cats Meow. Synthetic plush; gray felt paw pads & inner ear; painted face; glass eyes; jointed legs; swivel head; modern stuffing; holding mouse by tail.
Mint condition.
Paper tag. **$55-up (cat & mouse)**

Above right:
Marilyn Aston c1985
(The Hare Faire)
16in (41cm) Bear (*)
(*) Roaring 20s Bear. Brown frosted synthetic mohair; matching wool paw pads; plastic eyes; jointed legs & arms; swivel head; modern stuffing.
Paper tag. Mint condition. **$70-up**

Doris Beck c1986
18in (46cm) Bear
Burgundy mohair; matching ultra suede paw pads; black floss nose & mouth; black glass eyes; jointed legs & arms; swivel head; modern stuffing.
Mint condition.
Paper tag & medallion. **$125-up**

Carol Black c1987
   12in (31cm) Bear (*)
   4in (10cm) Dog (*)
   (*) Dorothy. White synthetic plush; tapestry paw pads; shoe-button eyes; jointed legs & arms; swivel head; synthetic stuffing; jumper & blouse; red lamé slippers with rhinestones.
   (*) Toto. Brown synthetic fur; glass eyes; not jointed; synthetic stuffing.
   Mint condition.
Paper tag (Bear). **$240-up (set)**

Below:
Catherine Bordi c1981
   14in (35cm) Bear (*)
   (*) Antique-style Bittersweet Chocolate Bear. Brown acrylic fur; matching ultra suede paw pads; plastic eyes; jointed legs & arms; swivel head; polyfill stuffing; #82 of 155.
   Mint condition.
Leather tag. **$185-up**

Debie Boulden   c1986
  24in (61cm) Rabbit (*)
  (*) Enchanted Rabbit. White
  synthetic mohair; artist-
  made eyes; plastic realistic
  blue lashes around eyes.
    Mint condition.
Brass tag.   **$1000-up**

Below:

Shirley Jane Boyington c1987
  10in (25cm) Bear (*)
    with Reindeer
  (*) Father Christmas. White
  mohair bear; sable-trimmed
  red velvet costume; glass
  eyes; jointed legs & arms;
  swivel head; limited edition
  10. Gray papier-mâché reindeer; painted eyes; not
  jointed.
    Mint condition.
No mark.   **$175 (set)**

Wendy Brent   c1986
20in (51cm) Bear (*)
(Rose Petal Dolls and Bears)
> (*) Orange Blossom, musical. Ivory-colored plush; wax padded nose with orange blossom scent; hand-blown blue glass German eyes; jointed legs & arms; swivel head; cotton stuffing; rose eyelet collar; music box plays, "Over the Rainbow."

Paper tag.   **$160-up**
Mint condition.

Opposite page—top left:
Verna Brightwell   c1986
(Bearly Makin' It)
> 12in (31cm) Bear (*)
> (*) Straw Bearie. Tan plush; strawberry-colored torso; yellow markings; black plastic eyes; jointed legs & arms; swivel head; modern fiber stuffing.
> Mint condition.

Paper tag.   **$45-up**

Opposite page—top right:
Regina Brock   c1985
> 7in (18cm Bear)
> Gold mohair (tufts of natural mohair sewn in sets of 3 stitches to create mohair); matching felt paw pads; shoe-button eyes; jointed legs & arms; swivel head.
> Mint condition.

Signed on foot.   **$185-up.**

Opposite page—bottom:
Barbara Burbeck   c1984
> 14in (36cm) Bear (*)
> (*) Christmas Teddy (left). Green mohair; black dralon paw pads; plastic eyes; jointed legs & arms; swivel head; synthetic cotton stuffing; original red ribbon & berries.
> Mint condition.

Cloth tag.   **$95-up**

Barbara Burbeck   c1985
> 16in (41cm) Bear (*)
> (*) Christmas Teddy (right). Red velvet plush; matching paw pads; plastic eyes; jointed legs & arms; swivel head; synthetic cotton stuffing; original white boa & Christmas greens.
> Mint condition.

Cloth tag.   **$95-up**

Phyllis Burkart   c1984
(Samshell Bear Co.)
          10in (25cm) Bear
Light brown synthetic mohair; black
pompon nose; plastic eyes; jointed legs
& arms; swivel head; original red suit.
      Mint condition.
Paper tag.   **$50-up**

Below left:
Georgia M. Carlson   c1985
(Barley Bruins)
          11in (28cm) Bear (*)
(*) Baby Bruins "Elite." Beige mo-
hair; black floss nose & claws; suede
paw pads; plastic eyes; leather eyelids;
jointed legs & arms; swivel head.
      Mint condition.
Leather tag.   **$95-up**

Below right:
Kit & Nick Chambers   c1985
(American Folk Bear Co.)
          12in (31cm) Rabbit (*)
(*) Velvet. Brown synthetic mohair;
pink yarn nose, mouth & whiskers;
plastic eyes; jointed legs; swivel head;
straw stuffing.
      Mint condition.
Paper tag.   **$85-up**

Sheila Clancy   c1979
Miniature Bear Muff
Pale gold mohair; flannel lining; black floss nose & mouth; glass stickpin eyes; swivel head; stuffed head.
No mark.   Excellent condition.   **$125-up**

Below left:
Liz Dahle   c1987
17in (43cm) Bear
Dark brown mohair & wool felt; shoe-button eyes; jointed legs & arms; swivel head; polyfill stuffing.
No mark.   Mint condition.   **$95-up**

Below right:
Steve Eberhart   c1986
19in (48cm) Bear
Brown frosted angora mohair; matching paw pads; rust floss nose & mouth; glass eyes; jointed legs & arms; swivel head; polyfluff stuffing.
Mint condition.
Cloth tag & paper tag.   **$135-up**

Rev. Chester Freeman c1983
10in (26cm) Bear
Carmel mohair; shoe-button eyes; jointed legs & arms; swivel head; modern stuffing; paper tag reads, "Baskets and Bears."
Mint condition.
Cloth tag & paper tag. **$75-up**

Diane Gard c1983
18in (46cm) Bear (*)
(*) A Bear with a Heart™.
Gray vintage alpaca; glass eyes; jointed legs & arms; swivel head; polyfill stuffing; limited to 500 pieces or 3 years.
Mint condition.
Cloth tag. **$100-up**

Above:

Dickie Harrison   c1984
3in (8cm) Bear (*)
(*) Modeled after a 1907 Bear in a Seymour Eaton book. Brown synthetic plush; glass monacled eyes; jointed legs & arms; swivel head; modern fiber stuffing.
Mint condition.

Paper tag.   **$75-up**

Dickie Harrison   c1984
3in (8cm) Bear (*)
(*) Modeled after a bear in a Seymour Eaton book. White synthetic plush; glass monacled eyes; jointed legs & arms; swivel head; modern fiber stuffing; #21 of 50.
Mint condition.

Paper tag.   **$75-up**

Left:

Betsy Hilgendorf   c1985
(The Purple Crayon Creations)
13in (33cm) Bear (*)
(*) Jailbear. Gray synthetic mohair; plastic eyes; jointed legs & arms; swivel head; modern day stuffing; plastic ball & chain; black & white striped costume.
Mint condition.

Cloth tag.   **$90-up**

Donna Hodges c1986
(The Heritage Bears)
12in (31cm) Bear (*)
(*) Jestbear. German mohair; ultra suede paw pads; glass eyes; jointed legs & arms; swivel head; modern stuffing; metallic silk jester costume. Excellent condition.
Cloth tag. **$175-up**

Below:
Lyric Johnston c1982
9in (23cm) Bear (*)
(*) Bear with Dolly-Face. White mohair; brown nose & mouth; Dolly-Face (Hilda); glass eyes (both); jointed legs & arms; swivel head; straw stuffing. Mint condition.
No mark. **$175-up**

Charleen Kinser c1987
(Forever Toys)
    25in (64cm) Bear (*)
    (*) Thaddeus P. T. Bear.
Light brown synthetic mohair; leather nose & paw pads; plastic eyes; jointed legs & arms; swivel head; polyester stuffing.
    Mint condition.
Cloth tag & paper tag. **$310-up**

John Knaggs c1986
    10in (25cm) Rabbit (*)
    (*) Baby Bunny. Light brown dralon; pink nose, mouth & inner ears; glass eyes; jointed legs; swivel head; cotton stuffing; tag reads, "Lovable Lasting Treasure."
    Mint condition.
Paper tag. **$70-up**

Charlene Kohler   c1986
(Bear Haven)
        16in (41cm) Bear (*)
        (*) Dorie, musical. Gold mohair; ultra
        suede paw pads, eyelids & inner ears;
        real hair eyelashes; plastic eyes; jointed
        legs & arms; swivel head; synthetic
        stuffing; clown costume.
                Mint condition.
Paper tag.   **$75-up**

Below left:
Ray & Christine Lamb   c1986
        15in (38cm) Bear (*)
        (*) Snow Bear. White synthetic mo-
        hair; matching leather paw pads; blue
        glass eyes; jointed legs & arms; swivel
        head; cotton stuffing.
                Mint condition.
Paper tag.   **$120-up**

Below right:
Cheryl Lindsay   c1987
(Elegant Fantasies)
        8in (20cm) Rabbit (*)
        (*) Babe. Brown mohair; no paw pads;
        glass eyes; jointed legs; swivel head;
        modern day stuffing.
                Modern condition.
Paper tag.   **$95-up**

Wendy Lockwood   c1985
13in (33cm) and
8in (20cm) Bears
Short gray plush; shoe-button-type eyes; jointed legs &
arms; swivel heads; fiberfill
stuffing.
Mint condition.
Cloth tag &   **$85-up (large)**
Paper tag.   **$35-up (small)**

Lynn Lumley   c1986
6in (16cm) Bear (*)
(*) Grandma Lund. White
llama fur; ultra suede paw
pads; glass stickpin eyes;
jointed legs & arms; swivel
head.
Mint condition.
Signed on foot.   **$125-up**

Above:
Mary Lynn   c1986
   7in (18cm) Bear
   Beige bear; ultra suede paw pads; glass
   eyes; jointed legs & arms; swivel head;
   synthetic stuffing.
     Mint condition.
Paper tag.   **$85-up**

Mary Lynn   c1986
   9in (23cm) Bear
   Long white mohair; matching felt paw
   pads; glass eyes; jointed legs & arms;
   swivel head; synthetic stuffing.
     Mint condition.
Paper tag.   **$85-up**

Right:
Chuck & Judy Malinski   c1984
(Judy K.M. Bears)
   13in (33cm) Bear (*)
   (*) Quint. Brown tipped synthetic mohair; brown velveteen-type paw pads;
   plastic eyes; jointed legs & arms;
   swivel head; new stuffing.
     Mint condition.
Cloth tag & paper tag.   **$95-up**

Karine Masterson c1987

12in (31cm) Bear (*)

(*) Rosebud. White synthetic mohair; plastic eyes; jointed legs & arms; swivel head; modern stuffing; flower in ear; limited edition 30.

Mint condition.

Paper tag. **$95-up**

Sarah McClellan c1982

14in (36cm) Bear (*)

(*) Toothy Teddy II. Rust brown synthetic mohair; molded tongue & teeth; cloth nails; glass eyes; jointed legs & arms; swivel head; modern stuffing; top hat; morning coat; plaid vest; holding cigar.

Mint condition.

Cloth tag. **$295-up**

Barbara McConnell   c1987
    18in (46cm) Bears (*)
(*) Whitney & Wendy. Tan mohair; glass eyes; jointed legs & arms; swivel heads; cotton stuffing; hand-knit sweaters & socks.
    Mint condition.
Gold heart in ear.   **$280-up each**

Below left:
Flora Mediate   c1986
(Flora's Teddys)
    14in (36cm) Bear (*)
(*) Hans Across Bavaria. Off-white mohair; plastic eyes; jointed legs & arms; swivel head; polyfill stuffing; blue leather-trimmed lederhosen.
    Mint condition.
Cloth tag & paper tag.   **$125-up**

Below right:
Erica McShad   c1986
    12in (31cm) Bear (*)
(*) Kleinhans. Tan synthetic tipped mohair; leather hand-stitched paw pads; glass eyes; jointed legs & arms; swivel head; modern fiber stuffing.
    Mint condition.
Paper tag.   **$70-up**

Gary & Margaret Nett 18in (45cm) Bear (*) c1987
 (*) Confederate Artillery Major, Civil War Series. Silver gray mohair; matching felt paw pads; glass eyes; jointed legs & arms; swivel head; straw & cotton stuffing; appropriate uniform.
Paper tag & booklet. Mint-in-box condition. **$250-up**

Gary & Margaret Nett 18in (45cm) Bear c1987
 Wool mohair; glass eyes; jointed legs & arms; swivel head; straw & cotton stuffing; wool costume; leather boots.
Paper tag & booklet. Mint-in-box condition. **$250-up**

Cathy Peterson   c1986
(The Roosevelt Bear Co.)
16in (41cm) Bear
Curly plush; rust twisted
floss nose & mouth; twill
paw pads; shoe-button eyes;
jointed legs & arms; swivel
head; polyfill stuffing.
Mint condition.
Leather tag.   **$150-up**

Robert Raikes   c1983
16in (41cm) Bear
White plush; hand-carved
wooden face & paw pads;
plastic eyes; jointed legs &
arms; wood fiber stuffing;
engraved on foot, "Raikes
#10."
Mint condition.
          $800-up

Janet Reeves c1986
12in (31cm) Bear (*)
(*) Clown Hug-A-Bear.
Pink, burgundy & ivory mohair; black nose & mouth;
shoe-button eyes; jointed legs & arms; swivel head.
Mint condition.
Paper tag. **$110-up**

Gloria Rosenbaum c1986
(Rosenbear Designs)
20in (51cm) Bear (*)
(*) Clown Bear, musical.
Poodle fur; suede leather
paw pads; plastic eyes; amber tears; jointed legs &
arms; swivel head; modern
stuffing; gold lamé, net &
lace costume; plays, "Bring
in the Clowns."
Mint condition.
$200-up

Kathy Sandusky c1987
(Bear Cupboard)
11in (28cm) Bear (*)
(*) October Birthday Bear.
"Rose quartz" hand-dyed
mohair; pink wool paw pads;
shoe-button eyes; jointed
legs & arms; swivel head;
cotton stuffing; gold necklace with birthstone.
Mint condition.
Paper tag. **$100-up**

Steve Schutt c1987
18in (46cm) Bear
Gray mohair; short sheared
muzzle & paw pads; shoe-
button eyes; jointed legs &
arms; swivel head; synthetic
stuffing.
Mint condition.
Paper tag. **$275-up**

Below:
Linda Spiegel c1982
(Bearly There)

16in (41cm) Bear (*)
(*) Clown. Brown plush; plastic eyes; jointed legs & arms; swivel head; foam stuffing; "made-on" pink & white costume.

Excellent condition.
Paper tag. **$65-up**

Below:
Linda Spiegel c1985
(Bearly There)

16in (41cm) Bear
Flowered tapestry; shoe-button eyes; jointed legs & arms; swivel head; modern fiber stuffing.

Mint condition.
Cloth tag. **$125-up**

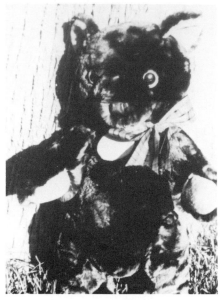

Gwyneth A. Taylor   c1985
  16in (41cm) Bear
  Dark brown seal fur; plastic eyes;
jointed legs & arms; wool fleece stuffing; medallion reads, "Gwynnie's
Bears//World's Best Bear//New Mex-
ico."
  Mint condition.
Leather medallion.   **$350**

Below left:
Pauline Weir   c1986
  12in (31cm) Bear (*)
  (*) Violet, (musical). Oatmeal colored
mohair; paw pads with tole painting;
glass eyes; jointed legs & arms; swivel
head; modern stuffing; matching dress
& bonnet; plays, "Be My Teddy
Bear."
  Excellent condition.
Ceramic ID.   **$160-up**

Below right:
Lynn West   c1985
(Lasting Endearments)
  22in (56cm) Bear (*)
  (*) King Rufus. Cinnamon brown synthetic mohair; black leather nose; glass
eyes; not jointed; modern day stuffing;
white bib with many pins & medals;
maroon velvet cape trimmed in "er-
mine," "jeweled" crown.
  Mint condition.
Cloth tag and paper tag.   **$850-up**

Averill   c1920
15in (38cm) Dog (*)
(*) Alley Dog (Humanized).
Black wool plush; brown
spot over eye & ear; composition head; painted eyes &
features; jointed legs &
arms; swivel head; kapok
stuffing.
Good condition.
No mark.   **$350-up**

Austrialian Mfg. Co.   c1980
8in (20cm) Australian Swagman
Plastic doll; white fur whiskers & eyebrows; painted
features; jointed legs &
arms; brown hat with 3
dangling corks to shoo flies
away; black bucket boots.
Mint condition.

c1980
11in (28cm) high sitting Koala (*)
(*) Musical. Wallaby & kangaroo skins; plastic claws &
nose; glass eyes; not jointed;
cork, styrene & flock stuffing; plays, ''Waltzing
Matilda;'' holding 11in
(28cm) sq. handkerchief
with painted tale of a swagman by Neil of Australia.
Mint condition.
Paper tag.   **$75 (set including
handkerchief)**

Above:
Baki c1986
12in (31cm) Bear
Gold mohair; plastic eyes; jointed legs
& arms; swivel head; wool-foam stuffing, tag reads "Baki//Plüschtiere."
Paper Tag.   Mint condition.   **$50-up**
£ 20-30
60-70 DM

Baki c1965
5in (13cm) tall,
7in (18cm) long Rabbit
Gray & white mohair; plastic eyes; not
jointed; kapok stuffing; tag reads,
"Baki//Plüschtiere."
Paper tag.   Good condition.   **$40**
£ 15-20
30-40 DM

Right:
Ballard Baines c1984
16in (41cm) Bear (*)
(*) Donovan. Rust colored velour;
black floss claws, nose & mouth; black
paw pads; plastic eyes; jointed legs &
arms; swivel head; gold heart attached
to chest; tag reads, "Ballard Baines
Bear Co."
Paper tag.   Mint condition.   **$150-up**

The Bear Factory   c1984
18in (46cm) Bear
Light brown frosted synthetic mohair; cotton paw pads & shorts; plastic eyes; jointed legs & arms; swivel head; modern stuffing.
Mint condition.

Paper tag.   **$45-up**

Bing Werke   c1920
20in (51cm) Bear
Gold mohair; tan wool felt paw pads; glass eyes; jointed legs & arms; straw stuffing.
Worn condition.

No mark.   **$1500-up**
£ 600-800
2000-2500 DM

Blue Ribbon Toy Co. (England)
c1950
14in (36cm) Bear
Tan mohair; inner ears & paw pads glow-in-the-dark; glass eyes; jointed legs & arms; swivel head; mouth opens when tummy is pressed; kapok stuffing.
Good condition.
Cloth tag. **$95-up**
£ 50-60
100-150 DM

Bruin Mfg. Co. c1907
13in (33cm) Bear
Black & tan mohair; floss nose & claws; shoe-button eyes; jointed legs & arms; swivel head; straw stuffing.
Excellent condition.
Cloth tag. **$750-up**
£ 200-250
400-500 DM

Canterbury c1979
24in (61cm) Bear (*)
(*) Canterbury Bear. Dark
brown mohair; suede leather
paw pads; plastic eyes;
jointed legs & arms; swivel
head; tag reads, "Canterbury, England."
Mint condition.
Cloth tag. **$400-up**

Carrousel c1982
18in (46cm) Bear (*) without hat
(*) Uncle Sam. Off-white
plush; glass eyes; jointed
legs & arms; swivel head;
fiberfill stuffing; limited
edition 200.
Mint-in-box condition.
Cloth tag. **$450-up**

Chad Valley   22in (56cm) Bear   c1927
    Tan mohair; black twisted floss claws; glass eyes; jointed legs & arms; swivel head; straw stuffing.
Cloth tag & button.   Mint condition.   **$800-up**
                                                                   £ 200-250
                                                                500-600 DM

Chad Valley   11in (28cm) Bear (*)   c1927
    (*) Clown. Gold & red mohair; gold flannel front paw pads; glass eyes; swivel head; not jointed; straw stuffing.
Button.   Excellent condition.   **$200-up**
                                                                   £ 80-100
                                                                300-350 DM

Opposite page:
Chad Valley   15in (38cm) Bear   c1950
    Gold mohair; heavily worked black nose; felt paw pads; glass eyes; jointed legs & arms; swivel head; kapok stuffing; tag reads, ''The Chad Valley Co. Ltd. by Appointment toymakers to H.M. Queen, Elizabeth the Queen Mother.''
Cloth tag.   Excellent condition.   **$250-up**
                                                                   £ 40-50
                                                                100-150 DM

Chad Valley c1948
18in (46cm) Bear
Gold mohair; black floss nose &
mouth; tan velveteen paw pads; plastic
eyes; jointed legs & arms; swivel head;
straw & kapok stuffing.
No mark.   Good condition.   **$275-up**
£ 80-100
100-150 DM

Below:
Chad Valley c1930
7in (18cm) tall Elephant
Green mohair; white felt tusks; brown
glass eyes; not jointed; straw stuffing.
Good condition.
Cloth tag & button.   **$100-up**
£ 40-50
80-100 DM

Chad Valley c1930
14in (36cm) Bear
Magenta mohair; black floss nose;
clear glass eyes; jointed legs & arms;
swivel head; straw stuffing.
Good condition.
Cloth tag & button.   **$600-up**
£ 200-250
600-800 DM

Character c1930

25in (64cm) Bear

Gold mohair; tan paw pads; glass eyes; jointed legs & arms; swivel head; straw stuffing.

Excellent condition.

No mark. **$500-up**
£ 200-300
400-500 DM

(Shown with Merry-Go-Round; see page 206 for description.)

Character c1935

17in (43cm) Bear

Dark brown mohair; tan cotton twill paw pads; black painted metal nose (worn); glass eyes; jointed legs & arms; swivel head; kapok stuffed body; straw stuffed head.

Excellent condition.

No mark. **$275-up**
£ 80-100
200-300 DM

Character   c1939
      12in (31cm) Bear
  White plush; black floss nose; white
felt paw pads; unusual glass eyes with
tiny white overlay glass (tear) in cor-
ner; jointed legs & arms; swivel head;
straw & kapok stuffing.
      Mint condition.
No mark.   **$100-up**
                    £ 30-40
                    50-80 DM

Below:
Character   c1940
    8in (20cm) & 15in (38cm) Bears
  These bears introduced Timme®, a
new fabric containing primarily mohair for children's toys. Tan Timme,
glass eyes, not jointed; foam stuffing;
tags include information about Timme.
      Mint condition.
Cloth tag & paper **$150 (larger**
tag.   **with tags)**
      $ 85 (smaller
          with tags)

Above:

Character c1940

9in (20cm) Elephant

Gray mohair; white felt tusks; glass eyes; not jointed; straw stuffing; red felt blanket & saddle.

Good condition.

No mark. **$100-up**

Character c1938

12in (31cm) Mouse (*)

(*) Timothy Mouse (Walt Disney Prod.). White velveteen; white cotton-gloved hands; celluloid "pie-eyed" eyes; not jointed; kapok stuffing; bandsman's costume.

Good condition.

Cloth tag. **$125-up**

Right:

Character c1940

24in (61cm) Panda

Black & white plush; black floss mouth; shoe-button eyes; painted metal nose; not jointed; head straw stuffing; body kapok stuffing.

Good condition.

No mark. **$75-up**
£ 20-30
50-100 DM

Chiltern c1938

10½in (27cm) Bear (*)

(*) Roly-Poly Bear. White mohair; glass eyes; not jointed; straw & kapok stuffing; makes sound when turned over.

Slight wear.

Cloth tag. **$65-up**

£ 40-60

80-100 DM

Below left:

Chips & Critters c1987

10in (25cm) Bear

Chain saw carved wood; natural finish; signed on base, "#1474."

Mint condition.

$100-up

Below right:

Clemens (Germany) c1962

35in (89cm) Bear

Brown mohair; tan wool felt paw pads; glass eyes; jointed legs & arms; swivel neck; straw stuffing; tag reads, "Clemens Germany."

Mint condition.

Paper tag. **$400-up**

£ 200-250

400-500 DM

Columbia c1907
19in (48cm) Bear (*)
(*) Roosevelt Laughing Bear. Rust mohair; tan paw pads; shoe-button eyes; jointed legs & arms; swivel head; straw stuffing; to make Bear laugh, press tummy or turn head.
Good condition.
No mark. **$700-up**
£ 100-150
300-400 DM

Below:
Commonwealth 1937-1941
14in (36cm) Bear (*)
(*) Feed Me Bear. Rust-brown plush; black floss nose; shoe-button eyes; not jointed; straw stuffing; bib not original; ring on back of head opens mouth to insert crackers, etc.; zipper in back opens to remove same from stomach; used in advertising animal crackers.
Worn condition.
No mark. **$300-up**
£ 40-60
100-150 DM

Dakin CL(*)

10in (25cm) Hand Puppet (*)

(*) Misha. Dark brown & cream-colored synthetic plush; plastic half-moon eyes & nose; not jointed; Olympic 5-ring belt; tag reads, "Misha™ © Organizing Committee of the 1980 Olympic Games in Moscow."

Mint condition.

Cloth tag. **$25-up**

Dean's c1985

14in (36cm) Bear (*)

(*) Schoonmaker Signature Series Bear. Re-issue of an early 1900s American Teddy Bear in honor of Patricia N. Schoonmaker's achievements in the Teddy Bear world. Pale gold mohair; matching flannel paw pads; black floss nose & mouth; plastic eyes; jointed legs & arms; swivel head.

Mint-in-box condition.

Cloth tag & paper tag. **$150-up**

Effanbee 1985
16in (41cm) Doll (*)
(*) Teddy Roosevelt. Vinyl; painted features; jointed legs & arms; swivel head; U.S. Army uniform; marked, "©1984 Effanbee//T. Roosevelt." Mint-in-box condition.

$150-up

Einco c1913
10in (25cm) Dog (*)
(*) Tubby. Gold mohair; brown tail, nose, mouth & lower back; red felt tongue; blown glass eyes turn from side to side; not jointed; swivel head; straw stuffing.
Mint condition with original tags.
Tags.

$165-up
£ 100-150
500-600 DM

Elka Toys (U.S.A.)   c1955
10in (25cm) Dog (*)
(*) Cocker Spaniel. Genuine
fur; plastic nose; glass eyes;
not jointed.
    Mint condition.
No mark.   **$100-up**

Elka Toys (U.S.A.)   c1958
14in (36cm) Dog (*)
(*) Poodle. Genuine fur;
plastic nose; open-mouth;
glass eyes; not jointed; straw
& kapok stuffing.
    Mint condition.
Paper tag.   **$100-up**

Erle (Germany)   c1950
32in (81cm) Bear
Red plush; white plush muzzle & inner ear; black floss
nose & mouth; white flannel
paw pads; glass eyes; jointed
legs & arms; swivel head;
straw stuffing; button reads,
"Erle Plushspielwaren."
Excellent condition.
Button.   **$125 up**
£ 20-30
800-100 DM

Fair & Carnival Supply
1907-1927
22in (56cm) Bear (*)
(*) Electric-Eyed Bear. Tan
mohair; white paw pads; tiny
light bulb eyes; jointed arms;
straw stuffing; white felt collar not original.
Excellent condition.
No mark.   **$700-up**
£ 100-150
400-500 DM

Fair & Carnival Supply   1907-1927
22in (56cm) Bear (*)
(*) Electric-Eyed Bear. Black mohair; black floss mouth; red yarn nose; white cotton covers paw pads; tiny light bulb eyes; jointed arms; swivel head; straw stuffing; button reads, "Teddy is good enough for me." T.R. photograph.
Slightly worn.

No mark.   **$750-up**
£ 250-300
650-750 DM

Below:
Farnell   c1936
13in (33cm) tall,
17in (43cm) long Dog
Cinnamon-brown mohair; short sheared muzzle & top of head; long ears; no paw pads; glass eyes; not jointed; straw stuffing; tag reads, "Farnell's Alpha Toys//Made in England."
Mint condition.

Cloth tag.   **$175-up**
£ 40-60
60-80 DM

Forbes Silver Co. (U.S.A.) c1907
2½in (6cm) tall Cup
Plated silver cup featuring 3 bears.
Good condition.
$135
£ 40-60
100-150 DM

Below:
Gebrüder Bing (Germany) c1905
12in (31cm) Bear
Copper-colored mohair; black floss
nose; four floss claws on each paw;
shoe-button eyes; jointed legs & arms;
swivel head; straw stuffing.
Good condition.
No mark.
$900-up
£ 150-200
600-800 DM

Gebrüder Bing (Germany)
c1905
18in (46cm) Bear
Gold mohair, glass eyes;
jointed legs & arms; swivel
head; straw stuffing.
Worn condition.
No mark   **$1500-up**
£ 150-200
600-800 DM

Gee   c1940
13in (33cm) Bear (*)
(*) Tumbling key-wound Bear. Gold
mohair; dark brown floss nose &
mouth; no paw pads; glass eyes; straw
stuffed head; mechanics in torso; tag
reads, "GEE tumbling toys//turn key
in direction of arrow."
Mint condition.
Cloth tag.   **$700-up**
£ 150-200
600-750 DM

Above:
Grisly c1985
6in (15cm) Bears
Red bear & green bear; mohair; no paw
pads; plastic eyes; foam rubber stuffing; tags read, "Grisly."
Excellent condition.
Paper tags. **$25-up each**
£ 8-10 each
20-30 DM each

Left:
Gund c1940
15in (38cm) Bear (*)
(*) Teddigund. Gold mohair; set-in
muzzle; white felt paw pads; glass
eyes; jointed legs & arms; swivel head;
straw stuffing.
Good condition; worn
muzzle & paw pads.
Cloth tag. **$275-up**

Gund c1930
11in (28cm) Santa (*)
(*) Musical. Celluloid face; black felt
boots; red corduroy suit & hat; painted
eyes; not jointed; kapok stuffing;
plays, "Jingle Bells."
Mint-in-box condition.
Cloth tag & paper tag. **$195-up**

Gund c1948
14in (36cm) Bear
Cinnamon plush; white
muzzle & inner ear; white
cotton paw pads; bakelite
nose; glass eyes; jointed legs
& arms; swivel head; straw
& kapok stuffing.
Good condition.
No mark. **$95-up**
£ 30-40
60-80 DM

Gund c1964
9in (23cm) Bear (*)
(*) Winnie-the-Pooh. Tan
plush; black set-in muzzle;
no paw pads on front paws;
yellow velveteen on feet;
glass eyes; not jointed; cotton stuffing; original sweater
& hat; manufactured in Japan.
Mint condition.
Cloth tag. **$55-up**

Gund   1983
7in (18cm) Bear (*)
(*) 85th Anniversary Bear.
Light brown synthetic mo-
hair; dark brown floss nose
& mouth; vinyl paw pads;
plastic eyes; jointed legs &
arms; swivel head; acrylic fiber stuffing.
    Mint condition.
Cloth tag & paper tag.   **$45-up**

Gund   c1928
15in (36cm) Rabbit,
excluding ears (*)
(*) Airplane Pilot. White
plush head, ears & hands;
muslin torso & legs; pink
floss nose & mouth; glass
eyes; not jointed; kapok
stuffing; pilot uniform.
    Mint condition.
No mark.   **$150-up**

Gund 1986
11in (23cm) Bear (*)
(*) Sears Winnie-the-Pooh
Centennial Bear. Gold plush;
red cotton twill mouth; black
tassel nose; red ribbed
sweater with "Pooh" on
front; black plastic eyes;
jointed legs & arms; polyester fiber fill stuffing; label on
sweater sleeve reads, "100
Years/Sears//1886-1986";
tag on bear reads, "Sears//
Winnie the Pooh//©Walt
Disney Productions."
Mint-in-box condition.
Two cloth tags. **$75**

Gund c1930
15in (28cm) Rabbit (*)
(*) Marine. Gold plush; for-
est green cotton body, shoes,
"mitten" hands & inner
ears; glass eyes; not jointed;
kapok stuffing; marine uniform.
Mint condition.
No mark. **$135-up**

Gund   20in (51cm) Rabbit   c1927
All-original Rabbit carrying lavender walking stick; clear glass eyes; arms wired for posing; swivel head; straw stuffing.
No mark.   Excellent condition.   **$145-up**

Gund   c1930
15in (36cm) Rabbit (*)
(*) Pirate. White plush head
& back of ears; glass eyes;
not jointed; kapok stuffing;
satin & velveteen costume.
Mint condition.
Paper tag.   **$135-up**

Gund   c1942
13in (33cm) Rabbit (*)
(*) Ride 'em Cowboy.
Plush; cowboy costume;
pink floss nose & mouth;
pink glass eyes with red
irises; not jointed; kapok
stuffing; hat ribbon reads,
"Ride 'em Cowboy."
Excellent condition.
No mark.   **$65-up**

Gund c1960
9in (23cm) Rabbit (*)
(*) Musical. White long pile plush; pink sateen inner ears; plastic eyes; not jointed; kapok stuffing; plays, Brahms "Lullaby."
Good condition.
Cloth tag. **$35-up**

Helvetic c1927
16in (40cm) Bear (*)
(*) Musical. Pink long curly mohair; matching wool felt paw pads; glass eyes; jointed legs & arms; swivel head; straw stuffing.
Good condition.
No mark. **$700-up**

Helvetic c1927
15in (38cm) Bear (*)
(*) Musical. Pale pink curly mohair; tan paw pads; glass eyes; jointed legs & arms; swivel head; straw & kapok stuffing; press tummy to activate music box.
Excellent condition.
No mark. **$1000-up**
£ 400-500
1000-1500 DM

Below:
Madame Hendren 1923
11in (28cm) Cats (*)
(*) Rare - Kitty-Puss (Humanized). Sateen fabric; painted features; hinged joints; kapok stuffing; cream-colored seersucker costumes; black tie slippers; tags read, "Kitty-Puss cries 'meow.'" Manufactured under special agreement with the artist Grace G. Drayton.
Mint condition.
Paper tag. **$400-up each**
£ 150-200 each
500-600 DM
each

Hermann c1924
20in (51cm) Bear
Gold silk plush; matching
cotton twill paw pads; glass
eyes; jointed legs & arms;
swivel head; straw stuffing.
Excellent condition.
No mark. **$700-up**
£ 80-100
200-300 DM

Hermann c1930
13in (33cm) Bear
White mohair; matching
paw pads; shoe-button eyes;
jointed legs & arms; swivel
head; straw stuffing. Painting by artist Carmella
Marchese.
Excellent condition.
No mark **$500-up (Bear)**
£ 200-250 (Bear)
600-700 DM (Bear)

Hermann c1949
16in (41cm) Bear
Unknown fabric; glass eyes;
jointed legs & arms; swivel
head; straw stuffing.
Excellent condition.
No mark. **$250-up**
£ 60-80
150-200 DM

Hermann c1955
17in (43cm) Bear
Tan mohair; black floss nose;
red felt tongue; Teddy baby
fore-paws; mohair paw pads;
open/closed mouth; glass
eyes; jointed legs & arms;
swivel head; straw & kapok
stuffing.
Good condition.
No mark. **$300-up**
£ 100-150
200-250 DM

Opposite page:
Hermann c1915
10in (25cm) Bear (*)
(*) Riding Bear. Tan mohair;
unusual seams on head;
glass eyes; not jointed; straw
stuffing.
Excellent condition.
No mark. **$500-up**
£ 200-250
500-600 DM

Hermann c1940
24in (61cm) Bear
Gold mohair; glass eyes; jointed legs &
arms; straw stuffing.
No mark.   Good condition. **$300-up**
£ 200-250
600-800 DM

Below left:
Hermann c1970
11in (30cm) Bear
Tan mohair; matching rayon jersey paw
pads; glass eyes; jointed legs & arms;
swivel head.
Mint condition.
Cloth tag & paper tag. **$175-up**
£ 30-40
70-80 DM

Below Right:
Hermann c1955
9in (23cm) Bear (in trunk)
Tan mohair; short-sheared muzzle;
glass eyes; jointed legs & arms; swivel
head; straw stuffing.
No mark.   Good condition. **$150-up**
£ 60-70
150-200 DM

Hermann c1949
27in (69cm) Bear
Dark brown mohair; cream-colored
sheared muzzle; tan felt paw pads;
glass eyes; jointed legs & arms; swivel
head; kapok stuffing.
Excellent condition.
No mark.   **$400-up**
£ 100-150
300-400 DM

Hermann c1984

11in (28cm) Cat (*)

(*) Oskar. Tan dralon; plastic nose & googly eyes; not jointed; foam stuffing; sailor costume with "M.S. Mary" on beret; tags read, "c Carlsen//Seebar//Copenhagen// P.I.B." & "Hermann Teddy Original//Seebar//Lizenz//. . ."

Mint condition.

Cloth tag & paper tag.	**$50-up**
	£ 30-40
	80-100 DM

(Shown with tall Horse Toy; see page 200.)

Hermann c1930

8in (20cm) Cat (*)

(*) Rare—Oskar. Composition head; gray flocked hair; white felt body; gray mohair tail & feet; painted eyes & whiskers; jointed arms; swivel head; kapok & soft filler stuffing; original clothes.

Mint condition.

Paper tag. **$1000-up**

Hermann c1982
12in (31cm) Monkey
Brown & tan mohair; white mohair
beard; brown air-brushing; plastic
eyes; jointed legs & arms; swivel head;
modern stuffing.
Button.   Mint condition.   **$65-up**
£ 30-40
60-80 DM

Below:
Hermann c1965
10in (25cm) Dogs (*)
(*) Poodles. White mohair; glass eyes;
metal noses; jointed legs; swivel
heads.
Excellent condition.
Tag.   **$65-up each**
£ 40-60 pair
120-180 DM pair

Hermann   16in (41cm) Monkey   c1949
Gold long synthetic fur; glass eyes; jointed arms and legs; swivel headstraw stuffed.
No mark.   Excellent condition.   **$250-up**
£ 60-80
150-200 DM

Hermann c1950
9in (23cm) Panda
String plush; black floss
nose & mouth outline; tan
wool felt paw pads & inner
mouth; glass eyes; jointed;
swivel head; kapok stuffing.
Good condition.
No mark. **$125-up**
£ 80-100
200-250 DM

Hermann c1957
12in (31cm) Panda
Black & white mohair; black
floss nose & mouth; open-
mouth; tan felt paw pads;
glass eyes; jointed legs &
arms; swivel head; kapok &
straw stuffing; cloth tags
read, "Hermann Original"
& "Federal Republic of Germany."
Mint condition.
Cloth tag & green **$300-up**
paper tag. £ 100-120
250-300 DM

Hermann   c1979
5in (13cm) Pony
Rust synthetic plush; black mane &
tail; black air-brushed hoofs; plastic
eyes; not jointed; modern filler stuffing; red plastic saddle; medallion, gold
with red letters.
Medallion.   Mint condition.   **$45-up**
£ 10-15
20-30 DM

Below left:
Hermann   c1955
4in (10cm) high,
6in (15cm) long Seal
Gray mohair; brown markings; brown
floss nose & mouth; glass eyes; not
jointed; straw stuffing.
Good condition.
Metal medallion.   **$50-up**
£ 10-15
20-30 DM

Below right:
Hermann   c1949
9in (23cm) Rabbit
Pale gold mohair; tan wool felt paw
pads; glass eyes; jointed legs; swivel
head; straw stuffing.
No mark.   Mint condition.   **$125-up**
£ 40-50
100-150 DM

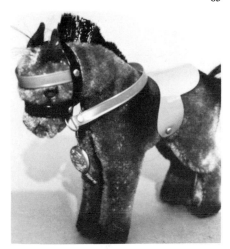

Hermann-Spielwaren c1963
19in (48cm) Bear
Gold silk plush; gold muzzle & paw
pads; black floss nose & mouth; glass
eyes; jointed legs & arms; swivel head;
straw stuffing; tag reads, "Hermann
Pluschtiere."
    Excellent condition.
Paper tag. **$100-up**
£ 40-60
60-80 DM

Below left:
Horsman c1909
12in (31cm) Billiken
Tan mohair Teddy Bear body; matching wool felt paw pads; painted eyes;
jointed legs & arms; swivel head; tag
reads, "Licensed Stamp//Copyr't
1909//by the// Billiken Co."
Cloth tag.   Good condition. **$350-up**
£ 100-150
300-500 DM

Below right:
Horsman Cop'rt 1911
8in (20cm) Cat (*)
(*) Pussy-Pippin (rare). Light brown
velveteen; painted "pie-eyed" eyes;
jointed legs; swivel head; cork stuffing.
No mark.   Excellent condition.   **$400-up**

Horsman 1911

    8in (20cm) Dog, sitting (*)
(*) Puppy Pippin. Cinnamon brown velveteen plush; composition painted head; black "pie-eyed" painted eyes; jointed legs & arms; swivel head; ruff not original; tag reads, "Puppy Pippin//Copyright 1911//By E.I. Horsman Co."

Cloth tag.   Good condition.   **$350-up**

Horsman c1911

    15in (38cm) Monkey (*)
(*) Ko-Ko, the Monkey with wind-up tin top (Humanized). Light brown; composition head; cloth body; painted features; jointed legs & arms; swivel head; straw stuffing.

No mark.   Excellent condition.   **$350-up**

Ideal c1905

24in (61cm) Bear
Gold mohair; tan flannel
paw pads; solid fabric nose;
glass eyes; jointed legs &
arms; swivel head; straw
stuffing.
Excellent condition.
No mark. **$900-up**
£ 150-200
400-500 DM

Ideal c1907

14in (36cm) Bear
Gold mohair; tan felt paw
pads; shoe-button eyes;
jointed legs & arms; swivel
head; straw stuffing; small
version of Ideal Smithsonian
bear.
Good condition.
No mark. **$700-up**
£ 200-250
500-600 DM

Ideal c1907

16in (41cm) Bear
Unusual light brown mohair with apricot tones; tan felt paw pads; twill fabric nose; glass eyes; jointed legs & arms; swivel head; straw stuffing.
Excellent condition.
No mark. **$800-up**
£ 100-150
400-500 DM

Below right:
Ideal c1907

18in (46cm) Bear
White mohair; tan felt paw pads; shoe-button eyes; jointed legs & arms; swivel head; straw stuffing; rare bear.
Excellent condition.
No mark. **$900-up**
£ 250-300
750-800 DM

Below left:
Ideal c1910

11in (28cm) Bear
Tan mohair; flannel paw pads; shoe-button eyes; jointed legs & arms; swivel head; straw stuffing.
No mark. Good condition. **$295-up**
£ 150-200
300-350 DM

Ideal   c1935
                18in (46cm) Bear
Cinnamon brown mohair; black floss
nose; tan felt paw pads; glass eyes;
jointed legs & arms; swivel head.
                Excellent condition.
No mark.   **$275-up**
                                  £ 100-150
                                  250-300 DM

Below left:
Ideal   c1910
                11in (28cm) Bear
Cinnamon mohair; no paw pads; mohair sewn in center of foot sole; black
fabric nose; glass eyes; jointed legs &
arms; swivel head; straw stuffing.
No mark.   Mint condition.   **$225-up**
                                  £ 60-100
                                  200-250 DM

Below right:
Ideal   c1910
                15in (38cm) Bear (*)
(*) Chester. Tan mohair; shoe-button
eyes; jointed legs & arms; swivel head;
straw stuffing.
                Excellent condition.
No mark.   **$700-up**
                                  £ 100-120
                                  300-400 DM

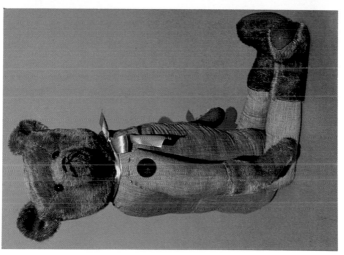

Ideal c1910

27in (69cm) Bear (*)

(*)Rare Bear Doll. Gold mohair head & paws (to elbows & shins); cotton fabric body; shoe-button eyes; legs & arms fastened to torso with metal buttons & pins; straw stuffing; child's clothes.

Excellent condition.

No mark. **$750-up**
£ 200-250
600-700 DM

Ideal   c1915
11in (28cm) Bear
Tan mohair; matching paw
pads; shoe-button eyes;
jointed legs & arms; swivel
head; straw stuffing.
Good condition.
No mark.   **$300-up**
£ 100-120
300-400 DM

Ideal   c1920
19in (48cm) Bear
Rare blue & gold mohair;
fabric solid nose; tan paw
pads; glass eyes; jointed legs
& arms; swivel head; straw
stuffing.
Excellent condition.
No mark.   **$700-up**
£ 100-150
300-400 DM

Ideal c1930

22in (56cm) Bear

White mohair; matching paw pads; glass eyes; jointed legs & arms; swivel head; straw stuffing.

Excellent condition.

No mark. **$400-up**
£ 200-250
500-600 DM

Below:
Ideal c1930s

19in (48cm) Bear

White plush; tan paw pads; black floss nose; black painted metal nose; glass eyes; jointed legs & arms; swivel head; kapok stuffing.

Excellent condition.

No mark. **$475-up**
£ 60-100
250-300 DM

Ideal   17in (43cm) Bear   c1939
Cinnamon red mohair; tan paw pads; glass eyes; gutta-percha nose; jointed legs & arms; swivel head; straw stuffed head; kapok stuffed body, original red bow.
Paper tag.

	Mint condition.	**$275-up with ID**
		£ 200-250
		400-500 DM

Ideal   15in (38cm) Bear   c1939
Cinnamon mohair; no paw pads; glass eyes; not jointed; swivel head; original red bow.
Paper tag on circus wagon card.   Mint condition.   **$275-up with ID**
£ 100-150
150-200 DM

Ideal   12in (31cm) Bear   c1939
Cinnamon mohair; no paw pads; black glass eyes; jointed legs & arms; swivel head; straw stuffed head; kapok stuffed body; original red bow.
Paper tag on circus wagon card.   Mint condition.   **$225-up with ID**
£ 100-150
150-200 DM

Ideal   10in (26cm) Bear   c1939
Cinnamon mohair; no paw pads; black glass eyes; not jointed; straw stuffed head; kapok stuffed body; original red bow.
Paper tag on circus wagon card.

	Mint condition.	**$100-up with ID**
		£ 80-100
		100-150 DM

Ideal c1905
20in (51cm) Bear
Tan mohair; shoe-button eyes; jointed legs & arms; swivel head; straw stuffing.
Excellent condition.
No mark. **$1000-up**
£ 250-300
400-500 DM

Below right:
Ideal 1953
26in (66cm) Bear (*)
(*) Smokey (1st version). Brown plush body, arms & legs; vinyl head, front paws & feet; inset plastic eyes; not jointed; kapok stuffing; hat not original.
Cloth tag. **$150-up**

Below left:
Ideal 1954
18in (46cm) Bear (*)
(*) Smokey (2nd version). Cinnamon brown plush; cream-colored front & inner paw pad; painted vinyl face; inset plastic eyes; not jointed; kapok stuffing; original vest & trousers.
Cloth Tag   Mint condition. **$100-up**

Ideal   17in (43cm) Bear   c1909
  Gold mohair; 4 black floss claws; glass eyes; jointed legs & arms; swivel head; straw
  stuffing; original mattress ticking fabric pants.
No mark.   Excellent condition.   **$900-up**
                                                                     £ 150-200
                                                                     500-600 DM

Ideal 1907-1927
19in (48cm) Bear (*)
(*) Electric-Eyed Bear. Black mohair; floss nose & mouth; tan paw pads; tiny light bulb eyes; jointed arms; straw stuffing; flag & sweater not original.
Excellent condition.
No mark. **$700-up**
£ 100-150
(See color photo on page 10.) 400-500 DM

Ideal c1910
12in (31cm) Bear
Gold mohair; matching paw pads; black floss nose & mouth; shoe-button eyes; jointed legs & arms; swivel head; straw stuffing.
Excellent condition.
No mark. **$225-up**
£ 100-150
250-300 DM

Ideal c1930

13in (33cm) Panda
Black & white plush; red floss tongue; glass eyes; jointed legs & arms; swivel head; kapok stuffing.
Good condition.

No mark. **$260-up**
£ 60-100
100-150 DM

Ideal c1915

14in tall,
9in wide Teddy Doll Muff
White mohair; tan felt feet & hands; painted face; not jointed; cotton padded & lined; reads, "Ideal//Baby Mine//U.S. Pat doll Muff #41179."
Excellent condition.

$250-up
£ 100-150
250-300 DM

King Features Syndicate   c1935
13in (33cm) Mythical Animal (*)
(*) Eugene, the Jeep. Composition;
painted yellow; red nose, cheek & ear
blushing; red navel; black eyes; jointed
legs & arms; swivel neck.
Mint condition.
No mark.   **$900-up**

King Features Syndicate   c1935
7in (18cm) Mythical Animal (*)
(*) Jeep. Composition; painted yellow;
red nose, cheek & ear blushing; red
navel; black eyes; jointed legs & arms;
swivel neck.
Mint condition.
No mark.   **$500-up**

Knickerbocker   c1930
15in (38cm) Bear
White mohair; white velveteen paw
pads; sheared muzzle; glass eyes;
jointed legs & arms: swivel head; straw
& kapok stuffing.
Excellent condition.
Cloth tag.   **$295-up**
£ 100-150
300-400 DM

100

Above left:
Knickerbocker   c1965
        15in (38cm) Bear
        White plush; white felt paw pads;
        white rayon string covering; red felt
        tongue; plastic eyes; jointed legs &
        arms; swivel head; head straw stuffing;
        body kapok stuffing; original Santa hat
        & bow.
                Excellent condition.
No mark.   **$125-up**

Above right:
Knickerbocker   c1930
        20in (51cm) Bear
        Cinnamon mohair; matching velveteen
        paw pads; black floss nose & mouth;
        glass eyes; jointed legs & arms; swivel
        head; straw stuffed head; kapok stuffed
        body; "S" stands for "Super Bear"
        embroidered by owner's grandmother.
                Worn condition.
No mark.   **$300-up**
                                  £ 100-150
                                  250-300 DM

Right:
Knickerbocker   c1972
        15in (38cm) Bear (*)
        (*) Smokey (Clifford Berryman face).
        Brown plush; pale yellow face; red felt
        tongue; plastic eyes; not jointed; syn-
        thetic fiber & foam stuffing; belt
        buckle reads, "Smokey."
Cloth tag.   **$95-up**

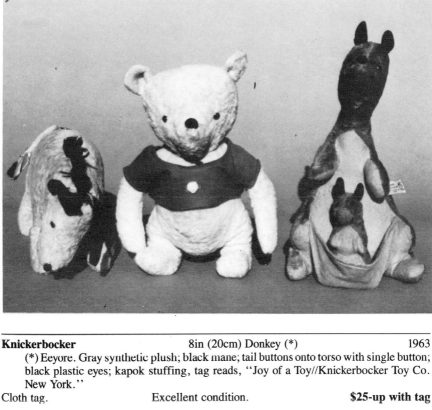

Knickerbocker   8in (20cm) Donkey (*)   1963
(*) Eeyore. Gray synthetic plush; black mane; tail buttons onto torso with single button; black plastic eyes; kapok stuffing, tag reads, "Joy of a Toy//Knickerbocker Toy Co. New York."
Cloth tag.   Excellent condition.   **$25-up with tag**

Knickerbocker   13in (33cm) Bear (*)   1963
(*) Winnie-the-Pooh. Gold synthetic plush; black tassel nose; red felt tongue; black plastic eyes; not jointed; kapok stuffing.
No mark.   Excellent condition.   **$75-up**

Knickerbocker   14in (36cm) Kangaroo (*)   1963
(*) Kanger. Brown synthetic plush back, head & tail; mustard-colored pouch; mustard-colored fleece fabric front, inner arms & inner legs; black plastic eyes, not jointed.
Cloth tag.   Good condition.   **$35-up**

Knickerbocker   6in (15cm) Kangaroo (*)   1963
(*) Roo. Brown synthetic plush; brown felt ears & tail; black felt eyes; not jointed; kapok stuffing.
No mark.   Excellent condition.   **$15-up**

Knickerbocker c1950
15in (38cm) Panda sitting (*)
(*) Pandora Panda. Black plush; black yarn "worked" nose & around open/closed mouth; cream velveteen paw pads, feet only; plastic eyes; not jointed; swivel head; kapok stuffing; cloth tag reads, "Pandora Panda//Trademark//N.Y."
Good condition.
Cloth tag. **$65-up**
£ 40-50
80-100 DM

L.B.M. Co. (retailer) c1907
Demitasse Spoons
Sterling silver. Left: Bear on handle top; "Teddy Bear" on tree trunk (stem); Billie Possum at tree base; bowl engraved with bear & possum; marked, "Sterling" & "Pa'd 07." Right: Bear on handle top; "Shelburne Falls, Mass." engraved in bowl.
Mint condition.
$100-up (left)
$ 75-up (right)
£ 15-20 each
80-100 DM each

Lenci c1984

14in (36cm) Panda

Black synthetic plush with white head & torso; plastic eyes; not jointed; modern stuffing; tag reads, "Certificate of Origine//Lenci//No 900124//Casa Fondata//Ncl 1919."

Mint condition.

Paper Tag. **$50-up**
£ 30-40
60-80 DM

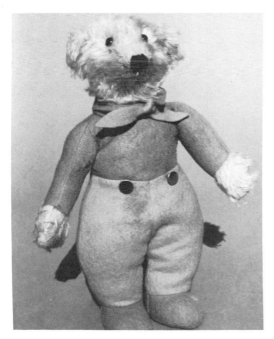

Little Folk c1982

12in (31cm) Bear

Gold mohair head & hands; "made-on" green felt top & shoes; orange felt trousers; back twisted floss nose & mouth; glass eyes; not jointed; straw stuffed head; remainder kapok stuffing.

Good condition.

No mark. **$100-up**

Armand Marseille c1907
15in (38cm) Doll (*)
(*) Eskimo Doll as Bunny. Bisque with jointed composition body; white painted hands; glass eyes; jointed legs & arms; swivel head; white fur bunny costume; "1894//A.M." on back of head.
Excellent condition.
$300-up
£ 100-150
500-600 DM

Fernand Martin (France) c1927
7in (18cm) Bear (*)
(*) Mechanical Bear. Tan woven fabric; metal nose, mouth, feet & hands; early glass eyes; not jointed; mechanical toy with incorporated key, when wound, bear sweeps with old broom he holds.
Excellent condition.
No mark. **$125-up**
£ 40-50
80-100 DM

Merrythought   15in (38cm) Bear   c1938
  Gold mohair; matching wool felt paw pads; black floss nose & mouth; glass eyes;
  jointed legs & arms; swivel head; straw stuffed head; kapok stuffed body; celluloid
  button with Merrythought logo in ear; signed by Oliver Holmes.
Cloth tag & button.   Excellent condition.   **$750-up**
£ 150-200
200-250 DM

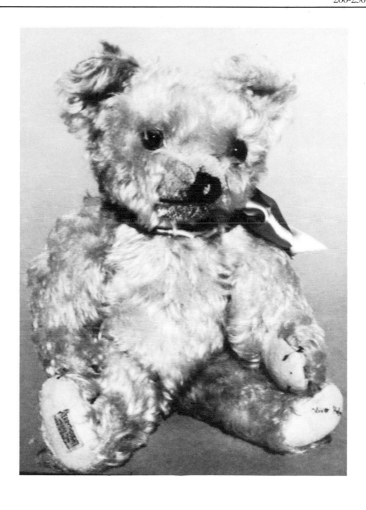

Left:
Merrythought   1984
18in (46cm) Bear (*)
(*) Edwardian Bear. Tan pure mohair; embroidered claws on paw pads; plastic eyes; jointed legs & arms; swivel head; #00651 of Limited Edition of 1000; yellow tag on foot reads, "Merrythought//Ironbridge Shrops//made in England."
Cloth tag.   Mint condition.   **$125-up**
£ 40-50
200-300 DM

Below:
Merrythought   c1984
18in (46cm) Bear (left)
Gold mohair; brown velveteen paw pads; plastic eyes; jointed legs & arms; swivel head; modern fiber stuffing.
Cloth tag.   Mint condition.   **$75-up**
£ 40-50
80-100 DM

Merrythought   c1984
15in (38cm) Bear (right)
Gold mohair; glass eyes; jointed legs & arms; swivel head; modern stuffing; tag reads, "Made exclusively for Harrods by Merrythought England."
Cloth tag.   Mint condition.   **$135-up**
£ 60-80
100-150 DM

(Shown with banner by unknown maker; see description on page 189.)

Merrythought 1983
11in (28cm) Bear (*)
(*) An English Rose Garden Bear.
White mohair; tan paw pads; plastic
eyes; jointed legs & arms; swivel head;
modern fiber stuffing; pink petals &
green leaves decorate head & neck;
International Bear Convention Teddy,
Calif., 1987.
Mint-in-box condition.
Cloth tag. **$95-up**
£ 20-25

Below:
Merrythought c1937
17in (43cm) long Dog (*)
(*) King Charles-type—nightdress
case. White mohair; black tail & ears;
glass eyes; head & legs partially straw
stuffed leaving lined area with zipper
for nightdress; zipper marked, "British."
Excellent condition.
$200-up
£ 40-60
150-200 DM

Merrythought   9in (23cm) Duck (Female)   c1965
Yellow nylon plush; orange felt bill; "made-on" shoes; brown velveteen skirt; white apron; plastic eyes; not jointed; synthetic foam stuffing; cloth tag on foot reads, "Merrythought Ironbridge Shrops Made in England."
Cloth tag.   Good condition.   **$50-up**
£ 20-30
30-40 DM

Merrythought   9in (23cm) Duck (Male)   c1965
Yellow nylon plush; orange felt bill; "made-on" shoes; brown trousers; plastic eyes; not jointed; synthetic foam stuffing; cloth tag on foot reads, "Merrythought Ironbridge Shrops Made in England."
Cloth tag.   Good condition.   **$50-up**
£ 20-30
30-40 DM

Merrythought c1935
29in (73cm) Bear
White mohair; glass eyes; jointed legs & arms; swivel head; straw & kapok stuffing.
Excellent condition.
No mark. **$800-up**
£ 250-300
750-800 DM
(See page 15 for color photograph.)

Mother Hubbard's Bear Cupboard 1986
10in (25cm) Bear (*)
(*) Mint Chocolate. Brown vintage mohair; glass stickpin eyes; jointed legs & arms; swivel head; antique lace-trimmed georgette lingerie.
Mint condition.
Paper Tag. **$120-up**

Merrythought   22in (56cm) Bear (*)   c1935
(*)Rare Two-faced Bear. Gold mohair; velveteen mask face on orangutan; brown velveteen feet; glass eyes; red felt nose; white worked "beanie;" labels read, "REGD. Design #83D499" and "REGD Design #801863," "Merrythought Hygienic Toys// Made in England."

Cloth tag & label.   Excellent condition.   **$3,000-up**
£ 800-1000
3000-4000 DM

Mutzi (Switzerland)   c1950
9in (23cm) Bear
White mohair; green glass
eyes; jointed legs; swivel
head; straw stuffed head; kapok stuffed body; original
clothes; tag reads, "Made in
Switzerland for J. W. Robin-
son—California."
Excellent condition.
Cloth tag.   **$275-up**
£ 100-120
200-300 DM

My-Toy Creation   c1950
23in (58cm) Bear (*)
(*) Berryman-type Walking
Bear. Brown & white plush;
black painted nose; flesh-
colored hands; "set-in"
muzzle; painted eyes; not
jointed; vinyl shoes.
Excellent condition.
Cloth tag.   **$100-up**

112

Nisbet c1980
15in (38cm) Bear (*)
(*) Angus, the Scott. Black
mohair & alpaca; brown
floss nose & mouth; black
vinyl paw pads; plastic eyes;
jointed legs & arms; swivel
head; red plaid vest & head
piece; tag reads, "Child-
hood Classics."
Mint condition.
Cloth tag. **$100-up**
£ 25-30

Nisbet c1980
51in (38cm) Bear (*)
(*) Paddy, the Irish Bear.
Green mohair & alpaca; tan
nylon paw pads; glass eyes;
jointed legs & arms; swivel
head; original red wool
scarf; Childhood Classic Series, #122 of 400.
Mint condition.
Cloth tag & paper tag. **$100-up**
£ 25-30

Above left:

Nisbet c1985

12in (31cm) Bear

Cinnamon brown British wool; black floss nose & mouth; plastic eyes; jointed legs & arms; swivel head; modern stuffing; signed on inside of original bib, "Jack Wilson June 1985." Mint condition. **$85-up**
£ 30-40
60-80 DM

Above right:

Nisbet c1985

15in (38cm) Bear (*)

(*) Bully Bear, Tribute to the late Peter Bull. Gold mohair; sweater replica of one of Peter Bull's hand-knit sweaters; plastic eyes; jointed legs & arms; swivel head; modern fiber stuffing; Limited Edition 5000 worldwide.

Cloth tag. Excellent condition. **$95-up**
£ 30-40

Noah's Ark c1920

14in (36cm) tall Bear

Hot Water Bottle

Pink rubber; painted eyes; printed on side, "Noah's Ark—Made in England.

Mint condition. **$125-up**
£ 20-40
80-100 DM

North American c1982
21in (53cm) Bear (*)
(*) Douglas Bearbanks. Smooth tan fabric; plastic eyes & nose; not jointed; modern stuffing; maroon jacket & cravat; gray striped trousers.
Mint condition.
Paper tag. **$40-up**

Pedigree (Ireland) c1935
24in (61cm) Golliwog
Cotton; red felt jacket; yellow vest; black felt buttons; plastic side-glancing eyes; red felt watermelon mouth; kapok stuffing.
Good condition.
Cloth tag. **$85-up**
£ 20-30

Pedigree (Ireland) c1955
13in (33cm) Bear
Gold mohair; brown velveteen ears; black floss nose; plastic eyes; jointed legs & arms; swivel head; bells in ears; squeaker; kapok stuffing; white felt collar; wearing Olympic pin worn by Irish athlete at the games.
Excellent condition.
Cloth tag. **$250-up**
£ 30-40
100-120 DM

Above:

Petz   c1925

3in (8cm) tall,
7in (18cm) long Polar Bear
White mohair; black floss nose &
mouth; glass stickpin eyes; not jointed;
swivel head; straw stuffing.
Excellent condition.

No mark.   **$100-up**
£ 60 80
200-300 DM

Petz   c1950

12in (31cm) Rabbit
Gold mohair; white chest, inner ear,
inside arms, legs & tail; black floss
nose & mouth; glass eyes; not jointed;
straw stuffing.
Mint condition.

Milk glass button.   **$125-up**
£ 30-40
100-150 DM

(Shown with Toy Duck; see page 205 for description.)

Above:

Raphael Tuck   c1908
Valentine
Paper; multi-colored lithograph; bear
with black painted nose & mouth;
printed on card, "Raphael Tuck Made
in Germany."
Good condition.   **$55-up**
£ 30-40
80-100 DM

Richardson, Frank C.A.   1910
15in (38cm) Doll (*)
(*) Teddy's Porter. Black cotton ribbed
fabric; black fur hair; brass nose ring;
metal and multi-colored beaded jewe-
lry; leopard loin cloth; shoe-button
eyes; not jointed; kapok stuffing. Richardson of Springfield, Ma. granted Design Pat. No. 40,722 for a Golliwog-
like creature commemorating T.R.'s
1909-1910 African hunting expedition.
No mark.   Mint condition.   **$400-up**

Above left:

Roullet & Decamps c1905
12in (31cm) Bear (*)
(*) Mechanical. Brown & white rabbit
fur; blue glass eyes; legs & arms
pinned to mechanical device for action;
papier-mâché molded body houses mechanical mechanism (arm keywind);
bear performs trapeze feats.

Excellent condition
(replaced stand)

Paper tag (possibly **$900-up**
auction). £ 400-500
750-800-up DM

Above right:

Roullet & Decamps c1902
11in (28cm) Cat (*)
(*) Mechanical. White rabbit fur; papier-mâché inner mouth painted red
with perfectly molded teeth; painted
pink papier-mâché nose; green glass
eyes; molded papier-mâché houses mechanical mechanism; winding keg activates Cat to open & close mouth,
"meow" & walk.

No mark. Mint condition. **$1500-up**
£ 200-400
800-1000 DM

Roullet & Decamps c1900
12in (31cm) Rabbit (*)
(*) Mechanical. White rabbit fur; black
fur tail; pink glass eyes; not jointed;
papier-mâché housing for mechanism;
rabbit knits & looks around when activated.

Mint condition.

"R.D." in key. **$1500-up**
£ 300-400
800-1000 DM

L.S. Scheffer c1914
9in (23cm) Rabbit (*)
(*) Rare Rabbit with bisque
face by J.D. Kestner. Pink
mohair; tan velveteen inner
ears; blue glass eyes; two
front teeth; not jointed.
Mint condition.
No mark. **$1800-up**
£ 300-400
1200-1500 DM

Schoenhut c1908
8in (20cm) Teddy Roosevelt
Rare; all-wood; painted yellow; carved & painted teeth,
mustache & glasses; brown
painted shoes; painted
glasses over eyes; spring
movement enables figure to
assume different positions.
Excellent condition.
No mark. **$900-up**

Above:
Schuco c1930
2¹/₂in (6cm) Bear
Pink mohair; tan felt feet & hands; black floss nose & mouth; tiny metal painted eyes; jointed legs & arms; swivel head; stuffed over a frame.
No mark.   Good condition.   **$100-up**

Schuco c1945
17in (43cm) Bear (*)
(*) Yes/No (Musical). Tan mohair; matching felt paw pads; glass eyes; jointed legs & arms; swivel head; medallion reads, "Tricky"; music box plays, "Oh Mein Papa."
Mint condition.
Medallion.   **$1100-up**
£ 400-600
1200-1500 DM
(See page 16 for color photograph.)

Above left:
Schuco   c1948
8in (18cm) Bear (*)
(*) Yes/No Bear (Humanized). Brown
mohair; glass eyes; jointed legs &
arms; swivel head; straw stuffing.
Excellent condition.
Medallion.   **$175-up**
£ 100-150
400-500 DM

Above right:
Schuco   c1950
19in (48cm) Bear
Cinnamon brown mohair; matching
paw pads; glass eyes; jointed legs &
arms; swivel head; straw stuffing.
Excellent condition.
No mark.   **$495-up**
£ 200-250
(Shown with Schuco Orangutan and Verhana
Hurdy-Gurdy; see pages 126 and 206 for descrip-
tions.)

Schuco   c1968
12in (31cm) Bear
Tan mohair ''made-on'' blue socks
with red edging; plastic eyes & nose;
wired; foam stuffing; soccer suit; removable shirt; plastic soccer shoes.
Paper tag.   Mint condition.   **$125-up**
£ 40-50
80-100 DM

Above:

Schuco c1930

5in (12cm) Perfume Teddy Bears
One red & one gold mohair; tiny
painted black metal eyes; jointed legs
& arms; swivel head; papier-mâché
form holds tiny perfume bottle.
Mint condition.

No mark. **$375-up each
(with original
bottle & stop-
per)**
£ 150-200 each
500-600 DM each

Schuco c1970

14in (36cm) Bear
Dark brown with "made-on" clothes;
plastic eyes & nose; not jointed; foam
stuffing.

Cloth tag. Excellent condition. **$85-up**
£ 20-30
60-80 DM

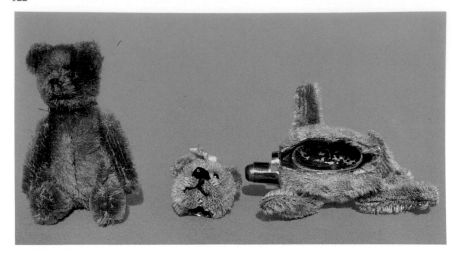

Above:

Schuco c1930

3¹/₂in (9cm) tall Teddy
Bear Compacts
One bright green & one lavender mohair covered compact; tiny painted metal eyes; jointed legs & arms; removable head to open.
Mint condition.

No mark. **$575-up each**
£ 200-250 each
600-700 DM
each

Schuco c1955

16in (41cm) Cat
Black mohair; ecru velveteen inner ears; red & white striped cotton covering torso; green glass cat eyes; on beadable wires (Schuco fashion) for posing; kapok stuffing; original clothes.

No mark. Excellent condition. **$85-up**
£ 30-40
40-60 DM

Above left:
Schuco c1930
> 5in (13cm) Cat Perfume Holder
> Pale gold mohair; pink embroidered
> nose & mouth; glass eyes; not jointed;
> removable head.

No mark.   Mint condition.   **$400-up**
£ 200-250
300-400 DM

Above right:
Schuco c1930
> 4in (10cm) Dog (*)
> (*) Yes/No Dog. Tan mohair; tiny
> painted metal eyes; jointed front legs;
> metal frame torso houses yes/no mech-
> anism.
>   Excellent condition.

No mark.   **$500-up**
£ 100-150
400-500 DM

Schuco c1970
> 15in (36cm) Dog (*)
> (*) Humanized Doxie. Light brown
> mohair; hard rubber nose; black floss
> mouth; plastic eyes; wired; original red
> sweater & green pants.
>   Excellent condition.

No mark.   **$100-up**
£ 40-50
100-150 DM

Schuco c1930
11in (28cm) Duck (*)
(*) Yes/No Duck. Fluffy yellow wool duck; orange bill, tongue & webbed feet; googly glass eyes; not jointed; swivel head.
Mint condition.
Paper tag. **$650-up**
£ 150-200
400-500 DM

Schuco c1948
9in (23cm) Elephant (*)
(*) Yes/No Elephant (Humanized). Pale gray mohair; googly glass eyes; jointed legs; swivel head; straw stuffing.
Excellent condition.
Medallion. **$300-up**
£ 100-120
250-300 DM

Schuco   c1965

11in (28cm) tall Mouse (*)

(*) Mechanical. Hard molded with synthetic mohair covering; glass eyes; wired; original clothes; mouse sweeps when tail is moved to & fro.

No mark.   Excellent condition.   **$95-up**
£ 20-30
40-60 DM

Below left:

Schuco   c1930

14in (36cm) Monkey (*)

(*) Yes/No. Light brown mohair; tan felt face; rayon fabric inner soles; glass eyes; jointed legs & arms; swivel head; straw stuffing; "made-on" jacket & hat.

Paper tag.   Mint condition.   **$400-up**
£ 150-200
500-600 DM

Below right:

Schuco   c1930

26in (69cm) Orangutan (*)

(*) Yes/No. Rust mohair; tan felt face, ears, hands & feet; glass eyes; jointed legs & arms; swivel head; straw stuffing; tail activates Yes/No motions.

No mark.   Good condition.   **$700-up**
£ 150-200
400-500 DM

Schuco   c1939

 8in (20cm) Orangutan (*)
 (*) Yes/No. Cinnamon
 brown mohair; felt face,
 hands & feet; glass eyes;
 jointed legs & arms; swivel
 head; straw stuffing.
 Excellent condition.

No mark.   **$350-up**
        £ 80-100
        200-300 DM

(For photograph see page 120 top right.)

Schuco   c1950

 3½in (9cm) Panda
 Black & white mohair; black
 floss nose & mouth; no paw
 pads; glass stickpin eyes;
 jointed legs & arms; swivel
 head; stuffed over frame;
 original red ribbon.
 Excellent condition.

No mark.   **$225-up**

Schuco   c1930

 3in (8cm) Pig
 Pink mohair; brown air-
 brushing; blushed pink felt
 snout, ears & nose; glass
 stickpin eyes; jointed legs;
 swivel head; stuffed over a
 metal form; original blue
 neck bow.
 Mint condition.

No mark.   **$250-up**
        £ 30-40
        100-120 DM

Schuco   14in (36cm) Rabbit (*)   c1930

(*) Yes/No. Tan mohair with red & white striped cotton legs; glass eyes; jointed legs & arms; swivel head; straw & kapok stuffing; original costume; tail activates Yes/No motions.

No mark.   Slightly worn.   **$400-up**
£ 100-120
400-500 DM

Schuco   c1950
10in (25cm) Rabbit (*)
(*) Yes/No Rabbit. Lavender mohair;
resembles W. Disney's "Thumper;"
plastic googly eyes; red plastic nose;
not jointed; yes/no swivel head oper-
ated by moving the tail.
Mint condition.
No mark.   **$275-up**
£ 60-80
300-350 DM

Below:
Schuco   c1958
15in (38cm) Rabbits
Tan & white mohair; glass eyes; bendable wired neck & legs; kapok stuffing;
costumes not original.
Excellent condition.
No mark.   **$145 pair**
£ 60-80 pair
120-150 DM pair

Schuco   c1950
   2in (5cm) tall,
4in (10cm) long Raccoon
Black & tan mohair; floss
nose & mouth; glass stickpin
eyes; jointed legs; swivel
head; stuffed over metal
frame.
   Excellent condition.
No mark.   **$150-up**
               £ 30-40
               100-120 DM

Simon & Halbig   c1909
   32in (81cm) Doll
Bisque head; long brown
hair; brown glass eyes;
"spring" strung composi-
tion body; incised,
"#1249" & "Halbig."
   Mint condition.
          $1600-up
          £ 600-800
          2500-3000 DM
(Shown with Steiff lamb; see page 167
for description.)

Steiff c1904
9in (23cm) Bear
Long tan mohair; black nose & mouth;
unusual head size & shape; shoe-button eyes; jointed legs & arms; swivel
head.
No mark.   Good condition. **$1000-up**
£ 100-150
300-400 DM

Below left:
Steiff c1905
10in (25cm) Bear
Tan mohair; shoe-button eyes; jointed
legs & arms; swivel head; straw stuffing; original clothes.
Mint condition.
Button (blank).   **$1000-up**
£ 600-700
2500-3000 DM

Below right:
Steiff c1905
10in (25cm) Bear
White mohair; light brown floss nose;
tan paw pads; shoe-button eyes; jointed
legs & arms; swivel head; straw stuffing; dress not original.
Excellent condition.
No mark.   **$1200-up**
£ 300-400
1000-1500 DM

Steiff   14in (36cm) Bear   c1905
     White mohair; light brown floss nose & mouth; tan felt paw pads; shoe-button eyes;
     jointed legs & arms; swivel head; straw stuffing.
Button.   Excellent condition.   **$2000-up**
                                                    £ 1000-1500
                                               2500-3000 DM

Steiff c1905

17in (43cm) Bear
White mohair; beige paw
pads; center seam on head;
shoe-button eyes; jointed
legs & arms, swivel head;
straw stuffing.
Good condition.

Button. **$3400-up**
£ 1500-2000
4500-5500 DM

Steiff c1907

4in (10cm) Bears
One gold & two white mo-
hair bears; no paw pads;
glass stickpin eyes; jointed
legs & arms; swivel heads;
straw stuffing.
Good condition.

Button. **$200 each**
£ 100-150
300-400 DM

Steiff   20in (51cm) Bear   c1905
Cinnamon brown long mohair; matching wool felt paw pads; center seam down top of
head; shoe-button eyes; jointed legs & arms; swivel head; straw stuffing.
Button.   Mint condition.   **$4000-up**
£ 2500-3000
7500-8500 DM

Steiff　　　　　　　　　　30in (76cm) Bear　　　　　　　　　　c1905

Off-white mohair; light tan paw pads; brown twisted floss nose; shoe-button eyes; jointed legs & arms; swivel head; straw stuffing; bow not original.

Button.　　　　　　　　　　Excellent condition.　　　　　　**$5500-up**
　　　　　　　　　　　　　　　　　　　　　　　　　　　　£ 1500-1800
　　　　　　　　　　　　　　　　　　　　　　　　　　　　6000-8000 DM

Above right:

Steiff c1907

12in (30cm) Bear

Tan mohair; matching paw pads; shoe-button eyes; jointed legs & arms; swivel head; straw stuffing; signed by Hans-Otto Steiff.

Button. Worn condition. **$800-up**

£ 200-250

600-800 DM

Above left:

Steiff c1907

12in (31cm) Bear

Long white mohair; light brown floss nose; shoe-button eyes; jointed legs & arms; swivel head; straw stuffing; working squeaker; shirt not original.

Worn paw pads.

No mark. **$1200-up**

£ 300-400

800-1000 DM

Steiff c1907

25in (63cm) Bear (*)

(*) Rare. Gold mohair; tan wool felt paw pads; shoe-button-type eyes; jointed legs & arms; swivel head; straw stuffing.

Excellent condition.

Button. **$5000-up**

£ 2000-2500

5000-6000 DM

(See page 17 for color photograph.)

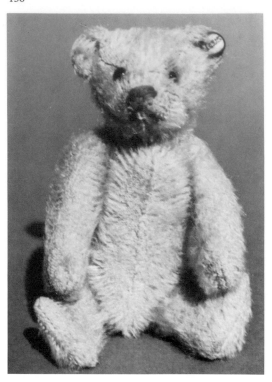

Steiff c1910

5in (13cm) Bear (*)

(*) Bear with rattle. White mohair; floss nose & mouth; no paw pads; glass stickpin eyes; jointed legs & arms; swivel head; straw stuffing. Worn condition.

Button. **$500-up**
£ 150-200
700-800 DM

Steiff c1927

16in (41cm) Bear (*)

(*) Musical. Blue long curly mohair; black floss nose; tan felt paw pads; over-sized glass eyes; jointed legs & arms; swivel head; straw stuffing; squeeze tummy to play music on bellows. Excellent condition.

No mark. **$800-up**
£ 250-300
800-1000 DM

Steiff   29in (74cm) Bear (*)   c1907
(*) Rare—Teddy G. White mohair; cream-colored paw pads; glass eyes; jointed legs &
arms; swivel head; straw stuffing.
Button.   Excellent condition.   **$12,000**
£ 5000-5500
10,000-12,000 DM

Steiff   c1927

     20in (51cm) Bear (*)
(*) Musical. Orange-tipped
gold mohair; beige paw
pads; glass eyes; jointed legs
& arms; swivel head; straw
stuffing; bellows music box.
     Mint condition.

Red cloth tag &   **$2000-up**
button.   £ 600-800
             2500-3000 DM

Steiff   c1930

     10in (25cm) Bear (*)
(*) Possibly Dicky Bear.
Off-white mohair; set-in
sheared muzzle; velvet paw
pads; glass eyes; jointed legs
& arms; swivel head; straw
stuffing.
     Worn condition.

No mark.   **$800-up**
           £ 350-400
           1200-1500 DM

Steiff 14in (36cm) Bear (*) c1930
(*) Teddy Baby. Pale gold mohair; matching felt paw pads; four black claws on each
paw; glass eyes; jointed legs & arms; swivel head; straw stuffing.
Red cloth tag & button. Mint condition. **$1000-up**
£ 400-500
1500-2000 DM

Steiff c1948
14in (36cm) Bear
White mohair; tan paw pads; glass eyes; jointed legs & arms; swivel head; straw stuffing.
Excellent condition.
No mark. **$450-up**
£ 100-150
400-500 DM

Steiff c1950
20in (51cm) Bear
White mohair; brown floss nose; tan wool felt paw pads; glass eyes; jointed legs & arms; swivel head; straw stuffing.
Excellent condition.
Button. **$900-up**
£ 300-400
1000-1400 DM

Steiff c1950

28in (71cm) Bear
Carmel long curly mohair; tan felt paw pads; glass eyes; jointed legs & arms; swivel head; straw stuffing; jacket & watch-whistle not original.
Excellent condition.
Button. **$1400-up**
£ 300-400
800-1000 DM

Steiff c1950

30in (76cm) Bear
White mohair; matching felt paw pads; heavy cardboard insoles for standing; glass eyes; jointed legs & arms; swivel head; straw stuffing.
Good condition.
No mark. **$1250**
£ 350-400
800-1000 DM

Steiff c1958

14in (36cm) Bear
Gold mohair; glass eyes; jointed legs & arms; swivel head; straw stuffing.
Excellent condition.
Button. **$450-up**
£ 150-200
300-450 DM

Steiff   9in (23cm) Bear (*)   1953
(*) Jackie, commemorating 50 years of bear making by Steiff. White mohair; brown
  floss nose with pink strand of floss across center; matching paw pads; glass eyes;
  jointed legs & arms; swivel head; tag reads, "Made in U.S. Zone Germany."
Cloth tag.   Excellent condition.   **$1400-up**
                                                                              £ 400-450
                                                                              1000-1500 DM

Steiff   c1953

13in (33cm) Bear (*)
(*) Musical. Gold mohair;
matching paw pads; brown
twisted floss nose; glass
eyes; jointed legs & arms;
swivel head; straw stuffing;
bellows music box activated
by pushing red felt circle on
stomach.

Good condition.

Cloth tag.   **$1000-up**
                    £ 250-300
                    1000-1500 DM

Steiff   c1955

3¹/₂in (9cm) Bear
White mohair; glass stickpin
eyes; jointed legs & arms;
swivel head; cloth tag reads,
"5310,04"; paper tag reads,
"Original Teddy."

Excellent condition.

Cloth tag, paper tag **$275-up**
& button.   £ 50-60
                    200-250 DM

Steiff   c1957
9in (23cm) tall Cat (*)
(*) Kitty Cat (standing/sitting). Gray & white striped mohair; long striped tail; pink floss nose & mouth; white whiskers; glass eyes; jointed legs; swivel head; straw stuffing.
  Excellent condition.
Button.   **$150-up**
                   £ 30-40
                   100-150 DM

Steiff   c1960
5in (13cm) Caveman (*)
(*) Neander. Mohair; red beard, whiskers, hair; plastic tooth; necklace; painted eyes; not jointed; tags read, "7755/13" and "Neander."
  Excellent condition.
Cloth tag, paper tag **$95-up**
& button.   £ 30-40
                   80-100 DM

Steiff   c1957
16in (41cm) Bear (*)
(*) Zotty. Brown frosted mohair; brown twisted floss nose; tan wool felt paw pads; glass eyes; jointed legs & arms; swivel head; straw stuffing.
Excellent condition.
Button.   **$350-up**
£ 100-150
200-250 DM

Steiff   c1950
29in (74cm) Bear
Frosted mauve long curly mohair; tan paw pads; dark brown floss nose & mouth; large glass Steiff eyes; jointed legs & arms; swivel head; straw stuffing.
Mint condition.
Button.   **$1450-up**
£ 600-800
1200-1500 DM
(Shown with Steiff Clownie; see page 155 for description.)

Above:
Steiff   c1960

13in (33cm) high,
26in (66cm) long Badger (*)
(*) Diggy. Light brown tipped dark
brown & white mohair; top of head
white; muzzle bottom, tummy & inner
legs brown; gray claws; plastic eyes;
straw stuffing.

Mint condition.

Cloth tag & button.   **$350-up**
£ 80-100
400-500 DM

Steiff   c1968

7in (18cm) Bear
Tan mohair; plastic eyes; jointed legs &
arms; swivel head; tag reads, "Original Teddy."

Mint condition.

Paper tag.   **$100-up**
£ 40-60
100-120 DM

Steiff   10in (25cm) Ape (*)   1972
(*) King Louie. Brown & orange dralon; orange hair; plastic eyes; not jointed; swivel head; foam rubber stuffing; tag reads, "0050/25."
Cloth tag, paper tag & button.   Mint condition.   **$150-up**
                                                              £ 60-80
                                                              100-120 DM

Steiff   16in (41cm) Bear (*)   c1970
(*) Baloo. Tan dralon; cream-colored muzzle & chest; white felt claws; plastic eyes; jointed arms; swivel head; foam rubber stuffing; tag reads, "0360.40//Baloo//W. Disney Prod."
Cloth tag, paper tag & button.   Mint condition.   **$400-up**
                                                              £ 60-80
                                                              300-400 DM

Steiff   8in (20cm) Elephant   (*)1973
(*) Baby Hathi. Gray dralon; felt ears & paw pads; long tan pile top-knot tail; plastic eyes; not jointed; straw & foam stuffing; tag reads, "0530/20."
Cloth tag, paper tag & silver button. Mint condition.   **$125-up**
                                                              £ 30-40
                                                              60-80 DM

Steiff   13in (33cm) Tiger (*)   c1973
(*) Shere Khan. Orange plush, dralon & cotton; plastic eyes; not jointed; swivel head; foam stuffing; tag reads, "0320/35."
Cloth tag, paper tag & button.   Mint condition.   **$175-up**
                                                              £ 40-60
                                                              120-150 DM

Steiff   10in (25cm) Ape (*)   c1980
  (*) King Louie. Black & cocoa dralon; rust hair; plastic eyes; not jointed; modern
  stuffing; tag reads, "King Louie//© W. Disney Prod."
Cloth tag, paper & button.   Mint condition.   **$100-up**
                                                                   £ 40-60
                                                                   100-120 DM

Steiff   11in (28cm) tall sitting Bear (*)   c1980
  (*) Baloo. Brown dralon; cream-colored muzzle & chest; plastic eyes; not jointed;
  modern stuffing; tag reads, "Baloo//W. Disney Prod.//#0380/28."
Cloth tag, paper tag & gold button. Mint condition.   **$300-up**
                                                                   £ 60-80
                                                                   250-300 DM

Steiff   10in (25cm) tall Panther(*)   c1980
  (*) Bagheera. Black plush; no paw pads; white muzzle; pink nose; plastic eyes; not
  jointed synthetic stuffing; tags read, "0381/25" & "Bagheera//© Walt Disney//Steiff//
  Knopf im ohr."
Cloth tag, paper tag & gold button. Mint condition.   **$175-up**
                                                                   £ 60-80
                                                                   100-150 DM

Steiff   8in (20cm) Elephant (*)   c1970
  (*) Baby Hathi. Gray dralon; tan paw pads; plastic googly eyes; not jointed; foam &
  synthetic stuffing; tags read, "Baby Hathi//©W. Disney Prod." & "0382/22."
Cloth tag, paper tag & button.   Mint condition.   **$100-up**
                                                                   £ 25-35
                                                                   50-70 DM

Steiff   1903
                 22in (53cm) Bear
Cinnamon brown mohair; shoe-button
eyes; jointed legs & arms; swivel head;
straw stuffing.
                 Good condition.
Button.   **$4500-up**
                                 £ 2500-3000
                                 7000-8000 DM

Below:
Steiff   c1958
                 18in (46cm) tall,
                 34in (86cm) long Ark
Gold wooden ark & house; painted red
trim; marked, "Steiff," "Knopf im
Ohr," & "Made in Germany."
                 Slightly worn,
            some minor pieces missing.
Printed   **$800-up**
identification.   £ 200-250
                                 1000 DM (mint
                                     condition)
                                 400-600 DM
                                     (incomplete)

Steiff   c1950

24in (61cm) Bear

Off-white mohair; matching paw pads; glass eyes; jointed legs & arms; swivel head; straw stuffing.

Some wear.

Button.   **$1000-up**

£ 200-250

600-700 DM

Above left:
Steiff   c1925
> 2in (5cm) tall Birds (*)
> (*) Bird's Wedding. Wool; glass stick-pin eyes; not jointed or stuffed; metal feet with "slip-on" slippers glued to green painted wooden base.
> Excellent condition.

Cloth tag & button.   **$250-up**
                           (complete set)
                           £ 100-150
                           400-500 DM

Above right:
Steiff   c1958
> 7in (18cm) Bird (*)
> (*) Bluebonnet. Mohair; yellow breast; blue wings, tail & top of head; white lower head and feather across wing; metal feet; hard rubber beak; shoe-button eyes; not jointed; swivel head; straw stuffing.

No mark.   Mint condition.   **$150-up**
                               £ 40-60
                               100-150 DM

Right:
Steiff   c1985
> 4in (10cm) Bird (*)
> (*) Adebar. White wool; black felt tail; orange plastic bill; red plastic feet & legs; glass stickpin eyes; not jointed.

No mark.   Mint condition.   **$15-up**
                               £ 10
                               15-20 DM

Above left:
Steiff 1986
3in (7cm) Bird (*)
(*) St. Valentine's Bird. Red & white;
black felt beak; glass stickpin eyes; not
jointed; Woolie stuffing; No. 1509/y.
Mint condition.
Cloth tag & paper tag. **$35-up**
£ 10-20
60-80 DM

Above right:
Steiff c1958
24in (61cm) Camel
Mohair; dark brown top of head, neck,
humps & tip of tail; air-brushed mouth
& hoof markings; steel frame; red &
yellow tassel; glass eyes; not jointed;
straw stuffing; cloth tag reads,
"#1360."
Mint condition.
Cloth tag & button. **$800-up**
£ 150-200
400-500 DM

Steiff c1925
12in (31cm) tall Cat (*)
(*) Puss in Boots. Off-white mohair;
pink floss nose; felt ears; "made-on"
red velveteen boots; beige felt paw
pads; white ruff; glass eyes; jointed
legs; swivel head; straw stuffing.
Excellent condition.
No marks. **$950-up**
£ 300-350
800-1000 DM

Steiff   c1913
8in (20cm) Cats
Game of Skittles (*)
(*) Rare. Gray felt cats in sitting posi-
tion on a pin; glass stickpin eyes; not
jointed; straw stuffing; red ribbon with
bell around necks; natural wood pines
with black edging.
Excellent condition.
$5000-up
£ 4000-up
4000-6000 DM set
600 DM each

Steiff   1926
3in (8cm) Cat
White velveteen; orange and black air-
brushing; glass stickpin eyes; not
jointed; straw stuffing; original ribbon
& bell around neck.
Excellent condition.
Cloth tag & button.   **$175-up**
£ 100-150
400-500 DM

Steiff c1926

17in (43cm) Cat (*)

(*) Studio Piece. Mohair; blue tipped fur on head back, sides & tail; white ears; pink floss nose & mouth; glass eyes; not jointed; swivel head; straw stuffing.

No mark.   Good condition. **$400-up**
£ 100-150
500-600 DM

Below left:
Steiff c1965

15in (38cm) Cat (*)

(*) Kalac (Humanized). Black mohair; red floss nose; pink inner ear & foot pads; white feet, hands, chest & tip of tail; plastic eyes; jointed legs; swivel head; straw stuffing.

Mint condition.

Cloth tag, paper tag & button. **$350-up**
£ 100-150
400-500 DM

Below right:
Steiff 1957 & 1958

13in (36cm) Chimpanzee (*)

(*) Chimpanzee, musical. Long brown mohair; tan face, ears, hands & feet; white beard; glass eyes; jointed legs & arms; swivel head; straw stuffing; press tummy for music.

Mint condition. **$1000-up**
£ 250-300
700-800 DM

Steiff c1959

40in (127cm) Clown
excluding hat (*)

(*) Studio Piece — Clownie. Rubber
head; glass eyes with thick floss lashes;
arms move back & forth only; station-
ary legs; straw stuffing; clown suit with
white felt gloves & red felt shoes; tags
read, "#7709/12" & "Clownie."
Excellent condition.

Cloth tag, paper tag & button. **$3500-up**
£ 500-up
2000 DM up

(For photograph see bottom of page 145.)

Top right:
Steiff c1977

6in (15cm) Deer (*)

(*) Bambi. Tan mohair & velveteen;
black air-brushed hoofs & ear tips;
glass eyes with oilcloth backing; not
jointed; straw stuffing.

Button.   Mint condition.   **$75-up**
£ 15-20
30-40 DM

Middle:
Steiff c1950

6in (15cm) tall,
12in (31cm) long Dinosaur (*)

(*) "Brosus" Brontosaurus. Tan mohair; black air-brushing; orange vertabrae; open/closed mouth; pink felt
inner mouth; glass googly eyes with
black pupils and green irises; not
jointed; straw stuffing.
Excellent condition.

No mark.   **$750-up**
£ 250-300
1200-1500 DM

Below right:
Steiff c1950

6in (15cm) tall,
11in (28cm) long Dinosaur (*)

(*) "Dinos" Stegosaurus. Tan mohair;
green air-brushing over back, head &
tail; green glass eyes with black pupils;
not jointed; straw stuffing.
Excellent condition.

No mark.   **$750-up**
£ 200-300
1200-1500 DM

Steiff c1950
8in (20cm) Dinosaur (*)
(*) Tyrannosaurus Rex. Tan mohair; black air-brushed circles; green air-brushing on back, tail & feet; green felt vertabrae; pink felt inner open/closed mouth; glass eyes; jointed arms; straw stuffing.
Excellent condition.
No mark. **$750-up**
£ 200-250
1200-1500 DM

Below:
Steiff c1913
8in (20cm) tall,
12in (31cm) long Dog (*)
(*) King Charles' Dog. White & black mohair; black floss nose & mouth; glass eyes; jointed legs; swivel head; straw stuffing.
Average condition.
Button. **$300-up**
£ 100-150
600-700 DM

Steiff   c1927
5in (13cm) tall Dog
Orange mohair (rare color); glass eyes;
not jointed; swivel head; straw stuffing.
No mark.   Good condition.   **$150-up**
£ 30-40
60-100 DM

Below:
Steiff   c1957
6in (15cm) tall,
8in (20cm) long Dog (*)
(*) Scotty. Black mohair; brown overlay on white glass eyes; not jointed;
swivel head; straw stuffing; red leather
collar; tag reads, "1314,0 Scotty."
Excellent condition.
Cloth tag, paper tag & button.   **$125-up**
£ 30-40
100-150 DM

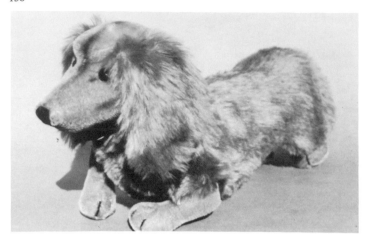

Steiff	11in (28cm) tall,	c1958

20in (51cm) long Dog (*)

(*) Waldi (Doxie). Copper brown mohair; short sheared on head, front legs, muzzle & back paws; long mohair ears; black twisted floss on claws & nose; glass eyes; swivel head; straw stuffing; tag reads, "#1302,02 Waldi."

Paper tag.   Excellent condition.   **$200-up**
£ 30-40
80-100 DM

Steiff	7in (18cm) tall,	c1958

9in (23cm) long Dog (*)

(*) Foxy. White mohair; black & brown air-brushing; glass eyes; not jointed; straw stuffing; red leather collar; tag reads, "Foxy."

Paper tag.   Excellent condition.   **$135-up**
£ 30-40
80-100 DM

Steiff   8in (20cm) tall,   c1958
10in (25cm) long Dog (*)
(*) Tessie (Schnauzer). Light silver-gray mohair; red felt tongue; felt inner ear; long whiskers; glass eyes; swivel head; straw stuffing; tag reads, "4320/22."
Cloth tag, paper tag & button.   Excellent condition.   **$135-up**
£ 30-40
80-100 DM

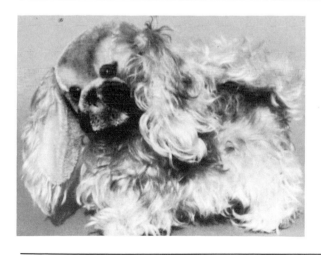

Steiff   9in (23cm) Dog   c1962
Pale gold to rust mohair; black muzzle; black floss nose, mouth & claws; glass eyes; not jointed; swivel head.
No mark.   Good condition.   **$75-up**
£ 30-40
60-80 DM

Steiff c1976

12in (31cm) Dog (*)
(*) Doxie. Rust dralon plush; very long ears; plastic eyes & nose; not jointed; synthetic filler stuffing.
Excellent condition.
Paper tag & button. **$95-up**
£ 20-25
50-75 DM

Steiff c1979

31in (79cm) Dog (*)
(*) Studio Piece — Red Setter. Cinnamon & reddish brown dralon; black nose; long pile tail & ears; plastic eyes; not jointed; straw stuffing.
Mint condition.
Cloth tag, paper tag **$600-up**
& button. £ 200-250
450-600 DM

Steiff c1979
31in (79cm) Dog (*)
(*) Studio Piece — Bosco,
Red Setter. Rust dralon; plastic eyes; not jointed; straw
stuffing.
Excellent condition.
Cloth tag, paper tag **$600-up**
& button. £ 150-200
500-600 DM

Steiff c1914
20in (51cm) Doll (*)
(*) Rare size. Flesh-colored
felt; center seam down face;
blue glass eyes; jointed legs
& arms; swivel head; straw
stuffing; all-original costume except skirt.
Excellent condition.
Button in ear. **$3000-up**
£ 1000-1500
3000-3500 DM

Steiff c1908
10in (25cm) Bear
White mohair; glass stickpin
eyes; jointed legs & arms;
swivel head; straw stuffing.
Good condition.
Button. **$900-up**
£ 400-450
1000-1500 DM

Steiff c1927

8in (20cm) Dog

White long curly mohair; black floss nose, mouth & claws; large glass eyes; not jointed; swivel head; straw stuffing.

Excellent condition.

Red cloth tag & button. **$350-up**

£ 60-80

400-500 DM

Below:

Steiff 1972

14in (36cm) long

10in (24cm) tall Dog (*)

(*) Rare 1972 Olympic Doxie, Bavarian mascot. Lavender, turquoise & light green dralon & cotton; black floss nose; plastic eyes; not jointed; excelsior stuffing; tag reads "4150/25."

Mint condition.

Cloth tag, paper tags & button.**$350-up**

£ 35-45

100-150 DM

Steiff c1979
> 31in (79cm) Dog (*)

(*) Studio Piece — Arco. Cinnamon dralon plush; tan face & legs; white chest; red felt tongue; glass eyes; not jointed; straw stuffing.
> Mint condition.

Cloth tag, paper tag **$600-up**
& button. £ 100-150
400-500 DM

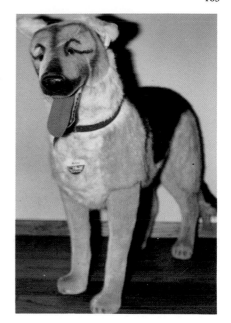

Below:
Steiff c1928
> 5in (13cm) tall Dog (*)

(*) Chinook (Byrd's Antarctic Expedition), rare. Off-white mohair; black mouth & paw pads; glass eyes; not jointed; straw stuffing; brown leather collar.
> Slightly worn.

Cloth tag, paper tag **$800-up**
& button. £ 250-350
600-800 DM

Steiff c1929

5in (13cm) Dog (*)
(*) Bully. White mohair;
black ears, tail & spots;
black floss nose & claws;
glass eyes; swivel head;
straw stuffing, tag reads,
"Steiff Original #3314
Made in Germany." Chil-
dren's book, *Bully & Mimi*,
written in Germany, 1931.
Mint condition (Dog).

Red Cloth tag (Dog).	**$400 (Dog)**
	$ 35 (Book)
	£ 200-250 (Dog)
	600-700 DM (Dog)
	£ 40-50 (Book)
	100-150 DM (Book)

Steiff c1928

4in (10cm) Dog (*)
(*) Bully. Off-white mohair;
orange ears, jowls & tem-
ples; glass eyes; swivel head;
straw stuffing.
Mint condition.

Red cloth tag.	**$300-up**
	£ 150-200
	500-600 DM

Steiff 1980

2in (5cm) tall,
2in (5cm) long Elephant (*)
(*) 100th year commemora-
tive Elephant. Bluish-gray
wool; gray felt ears; plastic
stickpin eyes; not jointed;
red felt saddle blanket. In Elephant's trunk is a plastic
box containing a scroll with
a gold seal concerning the
100th year.
Mint condition.

Button.	**$65-up**
	£ 20-30
	60-80 DM

Steiff   6in (15cm) Fox (*)   c1952
    (*) Xorry. Pale gold mohair; white chest, neck, inner ear & tip of tail; black floss nose;
no separate paw pads; glass stickpin eyes; not jointed; straw stuffing.
No mark.   Excellent condition.   **$50-up**
                                                       £ 25-30
                                                     60-80 DM

Steiff   5in (13cm) Fox (*)   c1960
    (*) Desert Fox or Xorry Fox. Gold mohair; white front; bushy tail with white tip; black
floss nose; glass eyes; not jointed; straw stuffing.
Button.   Good condition.   **$100-up**
                                                       £ 15-20
                                                     50-80 DM

Steiff c1968
11in (28cm) Giraffe
Gold mohair; orange spots;
plastic eyes; not jointed;
straw stuffing.
Excellent condition.
Button. **$65-up**
£ 15-20
30-40 DM

Steiff c1950
14in (36cm) Koala Bear
Pale gold mohair; open/
closed mouth; gray felt nose;
glass eyes; jointed legs &
arms; swivel head; straw
stuffing.
Excellent condition.
No mark. **$800-up**
£ 150-180
800-1000 DM

Above:
Steiff c1925

14in (36cm) tall,
16in (41cm) long Lamb
Lamb on wooden wheels. Off-white mohair, tightly curled; red floss nose; felt ears, muzzle & legs; glass eyes; not jointed; straw stuffed.
Good condition.
Cloth tag and button. **$800-up**
£ 300-400
1000-1500 DM

Steiff c1945

19in (48cm) Lamb (*)
(*) Studio Piece. White fleece; green glass eyes; not jointed; straw stuffing.
Mint condition.
Cloth tag & button. **$500-up**
£ 250-350
600-800 DM
(For photograph see bottom of page 129.)

Left:
Steiff c1972

65in (165cm) tall,
67in (171cm) long Mythical Llama (*)
(*) Studio Piece — Pushmi-Pullyu from movie *Doctor Doolittle*. White dralon; glass eyes; swivel necks; straw stuffing.
Mint condition. **$2500-up**

| Steiff | 12in (31cm) sitting Lemur (*) | c1982 |

13in (33cm) standing Lemur (*)

(*) Studio Pieces — Katta. Gray dralon & cotton; tan synthetic paw pads; plastic eyes; swivel head; wool foam & rubber stuffing; #0059/05 (sitting) & #0059/06 (standing). Cloth tag, paper tag & silver button. Mint condition. **$350-up each**
£ 100-150 each
400-500 DM each

Opposite page:
Steiff 1979
52in (132cm) Minute Man (*)
(*) Studio Piece. Synthetic velveteen; white shirt & vest; black boots; brown hat; orange trousers; gray gloved hands; black faille leggings; rust felt coat with satin lapels; brown glass eyes; brown realistic-looking synthetic hair; jointed legs & arms; swivel head; straw & modern fiber stuffing.
Mint condition.
Cloth tag, paper tag & button. **$3000-up**

Steiff   c1925
4in (10cm) Monkey
White mohair; flesh-colored
felt face, hands & feet; glass
stickpin eyes; jointed legs &
arms; swivel head; straw
stuffing.
Mint condition.
Cloth tag & button.   **$125-up**
£ 40-50
80-100 DM

Steiff   c1986
4in (10cm) tall Mouse (*)
4in (10cm) tail
(*) F.A.O. Schwartz
Christmas Mouse. Tan mo-
hair; felt tail & ears; glass
stickpin eyes; black bead
nose; not jointed; straw
stuffing; "jewel" decorated
metal crown; tag reads,
"#4308-05."
Mint condition.
Cloth tag.   **$65-up**
£ 40-50
100-150 DM

Steiff c1950
13in (33cm) Owl (*)
(*) Studio Piece — Wittie. Mohair;
mottled fur back; feather variance on
lower wings; expert air-brushing cre-
ates natural look; large lovely green
glass eyes; not jointed; swivel head;
straw stuffing.
Mint condition.
Cloth tag & button. **$350-up**
£ 40-60
100-150 DM

Below:
Steiff c1958
4in (10cm) Owl (*)
(*) Wittie. Mohair with felt feet &
wing tips; plastic eyes; swivel head;
straw stuffing; catalog #67b/4310.
Excellent condition/no I.D.
No mark. **$40-up**
£ 10-15
30-40 DM

Stelff c1958
8in (20cm) Owl (*)
(*) Wittie. Mohair with felt feet &
wing tips; plastic eyes; swivel head;
straw stuffing.
Good condition/no I.D.
No mark. **$100-up**
£ 20-30
60-80 DM

Steiff   c1950
6in (15cm) Panda
Mohair; black arms, legs, ears & chest;
white head; gray felt paw pads; black
floss nose & closed-mouth; glass stickpin eyes; jointed legs & arms; swivel
head; straw stuffing; original blue neck
ribbon.
Excellent condition.
Paper tag.   **$300-up**
£ 100-120
250-300 DM

Below:
Steiff   c1955
4in (10cm) Panda
Black mohair ears, legs & shoulders;
white head, chest & rump; black floss
nose & mouth; glass eyes; not jointed;
swivel head; straw stuffing; red collar.
Excellent condition.
Button.   **$100-up**
£ 25-30
80-120 DM

Steiff   13in (33cm) Panda   c1957

Long curly mohair; black legs, arms, ears & chest; white back, tummy & head; gray suede paw pads; closed-mouth; glass eyes; jointed legs & arms; swivel head; straw stuffing; catalog #5335,2.

Cloth tag.   Excellent condition.   **$750-up**

£ 200-250

600-800 DM

Steiff   8in (20cm) top of head to tail end Parrot (*)   c1972
(*) Lora. Mohair; red with yellow torso; blue on wings; white felt feet; green glass eyes;
not jointed; straw stuffing; tags read, "2520/12" & "Lora."
Cloth tag & paper tag.   Excellent condition.   **$95-up**
£ 30-40
100-120 DM

Steiff c1970
6in (15cm) tall Pigeon
Dralon; gray wings & tail;
pink plastic beak & feet;
black air-brushing; black
plastic eyes; not jointed;
straw stuffing; tag reads,
"#2565/25."
Excellent condition.
Cloth tag. **$95-up**
£ 20-30 (white or
gray)
50-75 DM (white
or gray)

Below:
Steiff c1913
16in (41cm) Polar Bear (*)
(*) Rare. White mohair;
matching paw pads; shoe-
button eyes; jointed legs &
arms; head not swivel but
moves freely; straw stuffing.
Good condition.
Button & **$1500-up**
remnant of £ 800-1000
white tag. 2000-2500 DM

Steiff c1932

5in (13cm) Rabbit
Off-white mohair; red floss mouth; glass eyes; not jointed; straw stuffing.
Excellent condition.
Button & fragment of red tag. **$250-up**
£ 60-80
300-400 DM

Below left:
Steiff c1923

11in (28cm) Rabbit
Short white mohair; pink inner ears; glass eyes; not jointed; swivel head; straw stuffing.
Slight restoration to ears.
Cloth tag & button. **$375-up**
£ 60-100
300-400 DM

Below right:
Steiff c1926

8in (20cm) Rabbit
White mohair; glass eyes; head rotates, activated by turning tail.
Cloth tag. Worn condition. **$700-up**
£ 150-200
600-800 DM

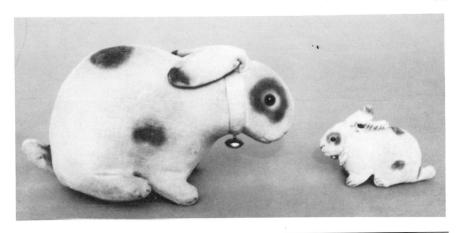

Above:
Steiff   c1929
4in (10cm) tall,
8in (20cm) long Rabbit
Off-white velveteen; rust air-brushed
spots; shoe-button eyes; not jointed,
straw stuffing.
Excellent condition.
No mark.   **$275-up**
£ 200-250
500-600 DM

Steiff   c1929
2in (5cm) tall,
4in (10cm) long Rabbit
White velveteen; rust markings; glass
stickpin eyes; not jointed; rattles when
shaken; paper tag reads, "Steiff Original Geschutzt 3404 Germany Importe-
d-Állemagne."
Excellent condition.
Paper tag.   **$250-up**
£ 150-200
400-500 DM

Steiff   c1939
5in (13cm) Rabbit
Pale gold mohair; glass eyes; not
jointed; swivel head; straw stuffing; tin
toy cart by J. Chein and Co., U.S.A.
Excellent condition.
No mark.   **$200-up (Rabbit)**
$ 45-up (Cart)
£ 30-40 (Rabbit)
60-80 DM (Rabbit)

Steiff   1939
9in (23cm) Rabbit (*)
(*) Girl (Humanized). Worsted wool;
pink floss nose & mouth; glass eyes;
not jointed; swivel head; all original
red, white & blue costume.
Excellent condition.
No mark.   **$150-up**
£ 60-80
250-300 DM

Steiff   1954
9in (23cm) Rabbit (*)
(*) Boy. Gray to white mohair; pink &
black floss nose; black floss mouth;
glass eyes; jointed front legs; swivel
head; straw stuffing; green felt "made-
on" pants; orange felt "made-on"
shoes.   ·
No mark.   Mint condition.   **$100-up**
£ 40-60
150-200 DM

Below:
Steiff
c1957
6in (15cm) & 10in (25cm)
Rabbits (*)
(*) Varlo. Dark brown mohair; glass eyes; jointed back legs; swivel heads; straw
stuffing.
No mark (smaller Rabbit).   Excellent condition.   **$ 85-up (smaller Rabbit)**
£ 30-40 (smaller Rabbit)
80-100 DM (smaller Rabbit)

Cloth tag & button   Excellent condition.   **$125-up (larger Rabbit)**
(larger Rabbit).   £ 40-50 (larger Rabbit)
100-500 DM (larger Rabbit)

Steiff   c1968
10in (25cm) Rabbit
Shaded gold mohair; black
air-brushing on outer ears
and on white mohair tail;
pink floss mouth; glass eyes;
bendable arms; straw stuffing; cloth tag reads,
"4325,00."
Mint condition.
Cloth tag & button. **$145-up**
£ 40-60
150-200 DM

Steiff   c1957
6in (15cm) Rabbit
Brown shaded to white mo-
hair; short sheared inner ear;
pink floss nose; glass eyes;
not jointed; swivel head;
straw stuffing.
Excellent condition.
No mark.   **$125-up**
£ 25-30
80-100 DM

Steiff   c1958
9in (23cm) tall,
6in (15cm) long Rabbit
Tan & gold mohair; light
brown air-brushing; red floss
nose; pink inner felt ear;
glass eyes; swivel head;
straw stuffing; original red
ribbon & bell; tag reads,
"#3318."
Mint condition.
Cloth tag, paper tag **$150-up**
& button.   £ 40-60
120-140 DM

Steiff   c1958
13in (33cm) Rabbit
Caramel mohair; white inner
ears, tail & neck; tan felt
front paw pads; glass eyes;
jointed front legs; swivel
head; straw stuffing.
Excellent condition.
No mark.   **$475-up**
£ 40-60
100-150 DM

Above:
Steiff   c1965
2in (5cm) tall,
4in (12cm) long Rabbit
Light tan mohair; white tail; pink floss
embroidered nose & mouth; plastic
eyes with black pupils; swivel head;
wood shaving stuffing.
Good condition.
No mark.   **$40-up**
£ 20-25
40-50 DM

Steiff   c1968
10in (25cm) Rabbit (*)
(*) Manni. Tan to white mohair; flesh-
colored felt open-mouth; pink floss
nose & mouth; brown air-brushed ear
tips; glass eyes; not jointed; swivel
head.
Mint condition.
Button.   **$150-up**
£ 40-60
80-120 DM

Steiff   13in (33cm) Rhinoceros (*)   c1950

(*) Rino. Light & dark brown mohair, black air-brushing; tan felt horn.
Button.   Excellent condition.

$225-up
£ 30-40
180-200 DM

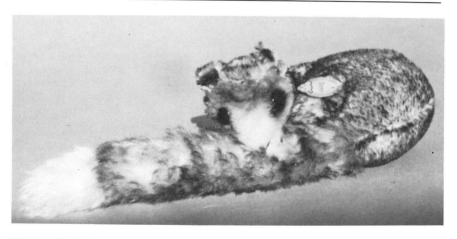

Steiff   8in (20cm) Rodent (*)   c1960

(*) Dormy, Rodent of Germany, (rare). Brown mohair; inset face; embroidered nose;
oversized plastic eyes; not jointed; tag reads, "Dormy."
Paper tag & button.   Excellent condition.

$100-up
£ 30-40
100-120 DM

Steiff   c1950

14in (36cm) Santa (*)

(*) Scarce size. Rubber head; flesh-
colored felt body; painted eyes; jointed
legs & arms; swivel head; straw stuffing; red wool Santa costume trimmed
with white wool fur.

Good condition.

Paper tag & button.   **$500-up**
£ 150-200
800-1000 DM

Steiff   c1950

12in (31cm) Bear

Gold mohair; matching wool felt paw
pads; glass eyes; jointed legs & arms;
swivel head; straw stuffing.

Button.   Good condition.   **$300-up**
£ 80-100
300-350 DM

Steiff   12in Santa   c1959

Rubber head; white plush beard & sideburns; painted eyes; jointed legs & arms; swivel
head; straw stuffed body; red wool Santa suit; red felt boots.

Cloth tag & button.   Good condition (head **$350-up;** £ 100-150; 400-500 DM.
slightly darkened).

Steiff   10in (25cm) Reindeer   c1950

Light brown mohair; tan felt antlers; black floss nose with single pink stitch; brown
glass eyes; not jointed; straw stuffing.

Cloth tag & button.   Good condition.   **$200-up;** £ 40-60; 80-100 DM.

Steiff c1950

3in (8cm) high,
4in (10cm) long Seal
Off-white dralon; brown air-
brushed spots & markings;
glass stickpin eyes; not
jointed; straw stuffing.
Excellent condition.
Button. **$85-up**
£ 30-40
40-60 DM

Steiff c1957

31in (79cm) Tiger (*)
(*) Studio Piece. Gold mohair; black air-brushed
markings; pink floss nose;
glass eyes; not jointed; straw
stuffing.
Excellent condition.
Cloth tag & over- **$1500-up**
sized button. £ 300-400
800-1000 DM

Steiff	13in (33cm) high,	c1978

21in (53cm) long Turtle Footstool

Mohair; plastic eyes; not jointed; straw stuffing.

Cloth tag & button.   Excellent condition.   **$250-up**

£ 80-100

200-300 DM

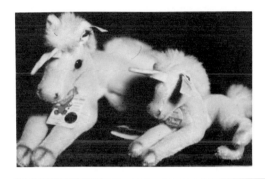

Steiff	6in (15cm) tall,	c1984

11in (28cm) long Unicorn

Light brown dralon; black eyelashes & hoofs; white twisted felt horn; royal blue plastic eyes; not jointed; Limited Edition 2000 pieces; tag reads, "0130/27."

Cloth tag, paper tag and gold button.

Mint condition.   **$95-up**

£ 20-30

80-100 DM

Steiff	5in (13cm) tall,	c1983

10in (25cm) long Unicorn

Light brown & white dralon; white twisted felt horn; deep blue plastic eyes; not jointed; synthetic filler stuffing.

Cloth tag, paper tag & gold button.

Mint condition   **$75-up**

£ 15-20

80-100 DM

Above:

Steiff c1970

23in (58cm) tall,
31in (79cm) wing span Vulture (*)
(*) Studio Piece. Tan dralon; brown
air-brushing; rubber bill & claws;
wings flap; glass eyes; not jointed;
swivel head; straw stuffing.
Mint condition.

Paper tag & button. **$900-up**
£ 100-150
600-800 DM

Steiff c1976

50in (127cm) George Washington
& 56in (142cm) high, 60in (152cm)
long Horse (*)
(*) Studio Pieces made for Bicenten-
nial, rare. Man: flesh colored synthetic
velveteen head; brown glass eyes with
overlay on white; pursed lips; expres-
sive facial expression; appropriate costume. Horse: white synthetic plush;
brown glass eyes; not jointed; straw
stuffing; leather saddle; leatherette
hoofs; metal stirrups.
Mint condition.

Cloth tag, paper tag **$6000-up**
& button. **George Washington**
& Horse)

Above:
Steiff   1948
    7in (18cm) Weasel (*)
(*) Minky. Off-white dralon; brown
air-brushing; black pupiless eyes; not
jointed; swivel head; synthetic filler
stuffing; tag reads, ''2230/22.''
        Excellent condition.
Cloth tag & button.   **$200-up**
                           £ 40-60
                           100-120 DM

Steiff   c1986
    3in (8cm) tall Wren House Bank
            with Bird
Wool bird; glass stickpin eyes; not
jointed.
        Mint condition.
Tag on bird house.   **$30-up**
                           £ 10-15
                           40-50 DM

Steiff   7in (18cm) Mickey Mouse (*)   c1930s

(*) Mickey Mouse. Black velveteen torso, legs & head back; "Mickey Mouse" hands; orange shoes; green velveteen short pants with "pearl" buttons; black painted mouth; "pie-eyed" oilcloth-type eyes; bendable arms; kapok stuffing; tag reads, "Mickey Mouse copyright Walt Disney."

Cloth tag, paper tag & button.   Mint Condition.   **$1500-up**
£ 500-600
1000-1400 DM

Unknown Maker   c1897
28 by 29in (71 by 74cm)
Banner (*)
(*) Memento for Victoria's
60 years reign as Queen.
Red, white, blue & brown
linen.
Mint condition.
$100-up
£ 40-50
100-150 DM
(For photograph see bottom of page
106.)

Right:
Unknown Maker   c1908
16in (41cm) Bear
American. White mohair;
brown floss nose & mouth;
tan paw pads; hump; glass
eyes; jointed legs & arms;
heavy cardboard in feet for
standing alone; straw
stuffing.
Good condition.
No mark.   **$800-up**
£ 200-300
700-800 DM

Unknown Maker   c1915
16in (41cm) Bear (*)
(*) Clown. Tan mohair head,
feet & hands; red & blue felt
sides; red & blue sleeves;
glass eyes; pinned legs;
straw stuffing.
Worn condition.
No mark.   **$225-up**
£ 40-50
80-100 DM

Unknown Maker   c1920
   24in (61cm) Bear (*)
   (*) Teddy Bear with Dolly-
Face. Cinnamon mohair;
glass eyes on bear head;
painted eyes on Dolly-Face;
jointed legs & arms; swivel
head; straw & kapok stuffing.
   Excellent condition.
No mark.   **$3000-up**
      £ 1000-1500
      4000-5000 DM

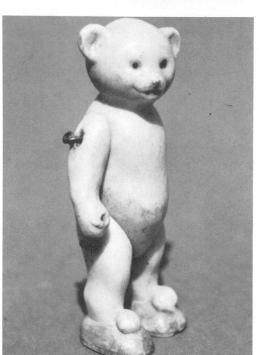

Unknown Maker   c1925
   3in (8cm) Bear
Bisque painted tan; arms &
legs "pinned" onto torso;
red painted tongue; lavender
painted shoes with pink
pompons; black painted
eyes; jointed legs & arms.
   Mint condition.
No mark.   **$250-up**
      £ 80-100
      150-200 DM

Unknown Maker c1925
18in (46cm) Bear (*)
(*) Rare. Gold mohair; tan
paw pads; celluloid eyes;
jointed legs & arms; swivel
head; straw stuffing; advertised and sold by National
Caraley Co.
   Good condition.
No mark. **$900**
£ 250-300
700-800 DM

Unknown Maker c1927
16in (41cm) Bear (*)
(*) Musical. Pink long curly
mohair; black yarn floss
nose & mouth; tan felt paw
pads; glass eyes; jointed legs
& arms; swivel head; straw
stuffing; squeeze tummy to
produce music on bellows.
   Excellent condition.
No mark. **$800-up**
£ 250-300
600-800 DM

Above:
Unknown Maker c1930
18in (48cm) tall,
22in (56cm) long Bear (*)
(*) Bear Velocipede. Brown mohair;
glass eyes; open-mouth with tongue;
not jointed; brown leather collar.
Good condition.
No mark. **$2000-up**
£ 300-350
800-1000 DM

Unknown Maker c1930
10in (25cm) Bear (*)
(*) Mechanical. Tan mohair; glass
eyes; mohair over papier-mâché frame
which houses mechanism.
No mark. Worn condition. **$100-up**
£ 40-50
80-100 DM

Unknown Maker   c1930
  18in (46cm) Bear
  Pink plush; tan wool felt paw
  pads; glass eyes; jointed legs
  & arms; swivel head; straw
  stuffing.
    Excellent condition.
No mark.   **$400-up**
                  £ 80-100
                  200-300 DM

Unknown Maker   c1930
  19in (48cm) Bear
  Possibly a "Fair Bear," a
  fair or carnival prize. Pink
  synthetic mohair; beige velvet paw pads; set-in muzzle;
  glass side-glancing eyes;
  jointed legs & arms; swivel
  head; straw stuffing.
    Excellent condition.
No mark.   **$175-up**
                  £ 60-80
                  200-250 DM

Unknown Maker (England)
c1945
28in (71cm) Bear
Beige mohair; beige felt paw
pads; pink ''made-on''
jacket with hood, can be
worn on head or as neck
scarf, non-detachable; glass
eyes; jointed legs & arms;
swivel head; straw stuffing.
Excellent condition.
No mark.   **$800-up**
£ 100-150
300-400 DM

Unknown Maker (Germany)
c1950
20in (51cm) Bear (*)
(*) Blue Fair Bear. Light
blue synthetic mohair; royal
blue paw-pads; glass eyes;
jointed legs & arms; straw
stuffing.
Good condition.
No mark.   **$45-up**
£ 100-150
400-500 DM

Unknown Maker c1958
19in (48cm) Bear
Synthetic mohair; glass
eyes; jointed legs & arms;
swivel head; modern stuffing.
Excellent condition.
No mark. **$65-up**
£ 40-60
100-150 DM

Unknown Maker c1960
15in (38cm) Bear
Tan plush; red wool felt lips
& inner mouth; plastic eyes
& nose; not jointed; stands
alone with front paws raised;
purchased in Amsterdam.
Good condition.
No mark. **$75-up**
£ 30-40
60-100 DM

Unknown Maker   c1952
11in (28cm) Bear
Bottle Holder
Pink synthetic mohair; black
floss nose & mouth; plastic
eyes; kapok stuffed head.
Excellent condition.
No mark.   **$50-up**
£ 40-60
80-100 DM

Unknown Maker   1904
6in (15cm) Convention Badge
Teddy Roosevelt pin at top;
miniature red, white & blue
flag; same colored faille ribbon; white fur-covered non-
jointed bear with glass stickpin eyes.
Excellent condition.
$375-up

Unknown Maker 13in (33cm) Cow (*) c1928
  (*) Pull Toy. Tan & white mohair; glass eyes; not jointed; when pulled by string under
  stomach, it moves its jaws & "moos."
No mark. Good condition **$400-up**
  £ 200-300
  600-800 DM

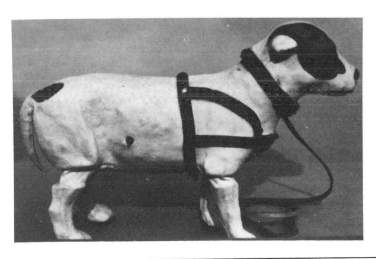

Unknown Maker (France) 12in (31cm) Dog (*) c1900
  (*) Mechanical. White fur; glass eyes; leather harness & leash; walks, turns head &
  barks.
No mark. Excellent condition. **$700-up**
  £ 250-300
  700-800 DM

198

Unknown Maker (Germany)   5in (13cm) tall,   c1950
11in (28cm) long Dog pulling Belltoy

    White dog; black ears; black floss nose & mouth; not jointed; straw stuffing; metal wheels with bell in center & rattle in each; marked inside of wheel, "Made in U.S. Zone Germany."

                       Excellent condition.   **$150-up**
£ 30-40
80-100 DM

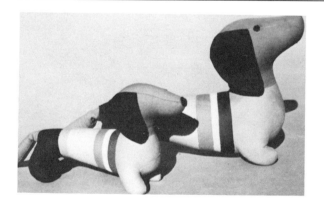

Unknown Maker   9in (23cm) & 6in (15cm)   1972
tall Dogs(*)

    (*) Munich Mascot, Doxie, 1972 Olympics. Linen hopsaking; 5 colors—lavender, yellow, blue, orange & green represent 5 Olympic rings; blue heads & tails; lavender ears; plastic eyes; not jointed; foam stuffing.

No mark.   Excellent condition.   **$100-up (larger Dog)**
$ 75-up (smaller Dog)
£ 30-40 (larger Dog)
£ 20-30 (smaller Dog)
50-80 DM (larger Dog)
40-60 DM (smaller Dog)

Unknown Maker   c1954

19in (48cm) Doll (*)

(*) Christopher Robin. Cotton cloth doll; painted features; jointed legs & arms; swivel head; kapok stuffing; original shirt and short pants; "Christopher Robin" on shirt.

Good condition.

No mark   **$125-up**

(Shown with Woolnough Bear; see page 207 for description.)

Below:

Unknown Maker   c1908

8in (20cm) tall,

10in (25cm) long Duck (*)

(*) Duck on Metal Wheels (Mechanical). Feathered felt; green head; yellow beak; blue, green & yellow wings; blue tail; glass eyes; not jointed; metal mechanism — when pulled, wings flap.

Excellent condition.

No mark.   **$400-up**
£ 80-100
200-250 DM

Left:
Unknown Maker 5in (13cm) Hedgehogs (Girl & Boy) c1950
  Felt body & "made-on" shoes; composition head; painted eyes; jointed front legs; swivel head; straw stuffing; boy in light brown shorts, pink vest, blue shirt; girl in striped cotton dress, tan apron.
No mark. Excellent condition. **$125-up pair**
£ 20-30 pair
40-60 DM pair

Unknown Maker 8in (20cm) tall Horse Toy c1920
  Tan felt stretched over frame of horse; glass eyes; not jointed; red painted platform with metal wheels.
No mark. Excellent condition. **$100-up**
£ 40-50
(For photograph see page 81.) 80-100 DM

Right:
Unknown Maker (Australia) 9in (23cm) Koala c1940
  White fur; black leather claws & nose; glass eyes; not jointed; straw stuffing.
No mark. Fair condition. **$35-up**
£ 10-15
30-40 DM

Unknown Maker   4in (10cm) sitting Koala   c1970
6in (15cm) high Koala Child's Purse
White & beige fur bear; black plastic claws & nose; glass eyes; not jointed; straw
stuffing. Natural fur purse; metal frame; plastic nose & eyes.
No mark.   Good condition.   **$75 (set)**
£ 25-30 (set)
80-100 DM (set)

Unknown Maker (Japan)   16in (41cm) Mickey Mouse and Minnie Mouse   c1982
(*) Opening memento for Tokyo Disneyland. Vinyl faces; white gloved hands & feet;
removable; painted facial features; not jointed; kapok stuffing.
Cloth tag & paper tags.   Mint-in-box.   **$75-up each**

Above left:
Unknown Maker c1940
(U.S.A.)
15in (38cm) Panda Doorstop
Genuine fur-covered form;
realistic plastic claws;
plastic eyes; not jointed.
Good condition.
No mark. **$275-up**
£ 60-100
150-200 DM

Above right:
Unknown Maker c1930
(Germany)
Pin Tray
Porcelain; painted green;
gold trim; features two
bears.
Mint condition.
No mark. **$75-up**
£ 40-50
120-150 DM

Unknown Maker c1939
9in (23cm) Pinocchio (*)
(*) Key wound. Painted tin;
turns in circles in shaking
motion when wound; printed
on back, "© 1939 Ent."
Excellent condition.
$200-up

Above:

Unknown Maker   c1930
    10in (25cm) Poodle Candy Container
        White fur over papier-mâché body;
        glass eyes; not jointed.
            Excellent condition.
No mark.   **$225-up**
                                  £ 100-150
                                  400-500 DM

Unknown Maker   c1908
    11in (28cm) Possum (*)
    (*) Billie Possum. Tan & gray mottled
    plush; shoe-button eyes; jointed legs;
    swivel head; straw stuffing; clothes not
    original.
No mark.   Good condition.   **$500-up**
                                  £ 150-200
                                  500-600 DM

Unknown Maker (Germany)   4in (10cm) tall,   c1930
8in (20cm) long Rooster & Cart
Tin Toy; multi-colored rooster; pink cart with white wheels.
No mark.   Excellent condition.   **$35-up**
£ 10-15
40-60 DM

(Shown with Hermann rabbit; for description see page 85.)

Unknown Maker   c1908
3in (8cm) Snow Baby Bear
Painted porcelain; brown head, hands
& feet; snow baby body; not jointed;
marked, "Germany."
Mint condition.   **$150-up**
£ 60-80
200-250 DM